Prayer Aflame: Prayer Prompts to Keep Your Prayer Life Energized

See You in the Morning, Volume 1

J. D. Alford

Published by J. D. Alford, 2024.

Table of Contents

I dedicate this book...

To Lord Jesus, without whom prayer would not be possible,

To my parents and grandparents, who showed me prayer by example,

To my truly devoted wife, Darla, who has been my encourager and partner in prayer,

To my sons, Stephen and Philip, who have encouraged me to put pen to paper and share these hopeful truths, and

To all the people in all the places where I have served who blessed me when I first learned and applied these principles in prayer.

To God be the Glory,

JDA

PRAYER AFLAME: PRAYER PROMPTS TO KEEP YOUR PRAYER LIFE ENERGIZED

First edition. September 1, 2024.

Copyright © 2024 J. D. Alford.

ISBN: 979-8-9899808-1-9

Written and compiled by J. D. Alford.

All Scripture is from the Holy Bible, authorized King James Version, Holman Bible Publishers, 1982, unless otherwise noted.

The author uses [brackets] within scripture to provide clarification or insight into definitions or ideas from the original language.

Recommended resource for reader: Strong's Exhaustive Concordance of the Bible: With Greek and Hebrew Dictionaries

Preface

I still vividly remember my childhood prayers on my knees alongside my mother just before I would go to bed. There are moments now when I wish that prayer and faith could be just that simple. I became a Christian at the age of nine. As I grew in Christ, so did my interest and approach in prayer. Seminars and studies at church expanded my understanding, and the length and depth of my prayers as a child and as a teenager deepened. College, church work, and seminary gave me even more insights into a world of prayer that I had never known or even imagined. My study as a pastor—both personal and professional—allowed me to walk with and be instructed by, what were to me, some of the heroes and giants in the faith. But something in the process has always drawn me back to the simplicity of what prayer should be. Ecclesiastes 5:2 advises that our words should be few. That takes some of the pressure off to be long and perfect. Perhaps our desire to do prayer "just right" has left us feeling inadequate to the point that we've simply lost hope or interest in prayer. Or both. My hope in this book is to ignite or rekindle your journey and passion in prayer. I've written this book with a perspective as if I were instructing my grown children and my grandchildren on how to pray. Sophisticated yet simple. Sophisticated in the sense of putting together all the best of my experiences of what to include in prayer but simple like the faith of those early bedside prayers. My goal is that, if you are new to prayer, you will begin to pray. And, if you're an old veteran in the faith, you will begin to pray with joy once more. There are many books that can be far more structurally complex (e.g., Peter Lord's *29/59 Plan*) and some more inspirational and exhaustive (*Best of E.M. Bounds*, R.A. Torrey's *How to Pray*, John R. Rice's *Asking and Receiving*). This book is designed to simply jumpstart your life of prayer. This book is not a full treatise on prayer. My goal here, again, is not to write about every nuance of prayer.

Thoughts, Thanks, Thistles

SO WHERE DID THIS IDEA for a book come from? My journey in restarting my own prayer life came about when things were in a lull. It was when there wasn't anything good or bad necessarily going on, just the normal events of life seemed to be just lifeless. In fact, it seemed like it may have happened as a result of what could be described as just one-time circumstances. As I was sensing a desire for a deeper or rekindled experience with God, I gradually noticed that I would read and reflect and at times pray in my quiet time devotionals. I began to find myself coming across some great truths that propelled me to keep prayer going. I suddenly felt compelled to write some of these things down. I had a little ledger book which I was no longer using where I had accounted a few financial things. You know how it is, right? Living in an ever increasing less-paper-more-digital world, I really didn't need to account for money that way anymore. That gave me the thought that I could write some meaningful verses down in the old financial journal. Over time, I started dividing the ledger book into categories to record my insights. As I would discover great thoughts about who God is, I wrote those into a section called "Thoughts on God". In another section, I collected the verses about the good and gracious acts of God and called it "Thanks." Lastly, I entitled the section where I would pray for others, "Thorns and Thistles." You know, those prickly situations in our lives that required us to look to and rely on God's promises. If you are unaware, a thistle is a beautiful purple but prickly type plant. Many of our most difficult problems are like that—lovely and lousy—mixed together into a prickly mess. It is out of that many years' process that this book on prayer has emerged. My hope is that you engage your most profound thoughts, deepest thanks and your greatest victories over the thorns and thistles in your life and begin to pray afresh and anew.

Introduction

It seems that in every generation there needs to be a reset on spiritual things. There are so many significant spiritual disciplines, it's easy to imagine someone asking, "Where is the best place to begin?" I believe that prayer is the best place to begin a journey of renewal. Prayer is one of the most essential—if not the absolute center—of what it means to be a believer. You cannot be a believer without asking God to save you. The act of asking God to save you is prayer. So, if over time, prayer has become only an interesting concept or a boring, lifeless exercise in its appeal or practice, then this book is for you.

For many, prayer is a nonstarter. It's not that people don't need a touch of the Almighty, it's just that there is a built-up resistance toward talking to God. For example, some people believe themselves to be atheist (don't believe) or agnostic (not knowing) if God exists. Prayer to them is not only a waste of time but is also ludicrous. So, for prayer to come alive, you must have some measure of belief or faith in the God you are praying to. Hebrews 11:6 commands, *"But without faith it is impossible to please Him: for he that cometh to God must believe that He [God] is, and that He [God] is a rewarder of them that diligently seek him."*

Imagine that you have a car that has a weak battery. Every day when you go to start it, you can tell that it has a little more trouble every time. Let's further imagine that you sometimes don't even start the car at all. Do you know that there are many parts of your modern car that are working even when you're not in it? Things like your clock and security system, etc., are running even when your car isn't. There is an unseen drain. Over time the battery weakens until some cold morning you walk out, turn the key, and nothing happens. No spark, no fire, no nothing. What are you to do? You don't need an overhaul—you need a jumpstart from a stronger battery. You hook up only to the stronger battery with some cables. Still nothing of course because there is still no connection (but there is hope!). The power hasn't and cannot yet be transferred. You then put the neutral/negative cable onto the ground of the impaired car, then place the positive/hot (usually red) and you may hear the car with the dead battery start to show signs of life. Lights come on a few sensors ding. There is hope, even though the car has yet to start. The impaired car is only accessing the good battery's power. Then the moment of truth. You turn the switch and *voila* you start the engine. Now, the old battery still must charge before it is truly good to go. If there are no real issues with the vehicle, it will charge just by running the car. You're in business. Unless you don't fire up the car again for an extended period of time. Think of this book as a jumpstart. The fact that you are interested is like putting one cable on. The fact that you are responding to the power and pull of the Holy Spirit is another cable upon which—when you act by faith—you hear some hopeful signals. All that is left to do is to turn the key and pray. Let this book be the key to get you praying again. Prayer by itself will begin to energize you and your desire to pray more.

The Bible makes it clear. You get out of prayer based on your belief before you start to pray. In Matthew 17:20, Jesus indicated that—if you had the amount of faith of the size of the tiny mustard seed—it would have the equivalent power to move a mountain. In essence, if we take a step of faith to believe in an activity like prayer, God will more than compensate that tiny amount of faith with a far greater positive effect. God will ignite our prayers by our faith to connect up and begin.

So, let's get to the heart of why you are interested in prayer but are not really praying. Think for just a moment. What have you heard or believed that would cause you to think you can't pray, shouldn't pray, or that prayer would not be heard or would be ineffective? Beyond what your objections or hesitations might be, consider this, in Luke 18:1 the writer, Luke, says *"And He [Jesus] spake a parable unto them to his end, that men ought always to pray, and not to faint."* Bottom line? Jesus, God and Savior and Lord, says you should pray. He didn't put any restrictions on it. When the thief on the cross asked Jesus to remember him when He went to paradise, Jesus listened! In Jesus' estimation, it's worth your time and effort. Always. In good times and bad. Even in the Old Testament we see the unwilling, hesitant prophet Jonah go to the non-Israelite city of Nineveh and see God do a mighty work with people in an unexpected way. God heard their prayer! God was concerned about them and was working in their midst. He heard their prayers, saw their need, and sent His prophet to speak to them and guide them. God wants to speak to us. So, will you believe Jesus or believe the built-up reasons of your own thinking that are causing you to not engage in prayer?

Another question which might throw up a roadblock to your praying is, "What have I said or done that causes me to think I'm now somehow disqualified to pray or speak to God?" I would invite you to hear the message of Romans 8:1, *"There is therefore now no condemnation to them which are in Christ Jesus, who walk not after the flesh, but after the Spirit."* The fact that you have an interest in prayer is the work of the Holy Spirit of God! After believing in God's forgiveness of sin by the sacrifice of Jesus, you cannot be condemned. This truth is affirmed many times in the Bible. When God makes a promise, He keeps it! See II Timothy 2:13, "If we believe not, yet He [God] *abideth faithful: he cannot deny himself."* God will not go back on His word. We stand before Him clean. That's not to say that we will not make mistakes and even drift from our closeness to God. Maybe even feel bad for it. In those instances, when we realize this distant feeling, even then God has a word for our anxious, doubting heart of feelings. In I John 3:19-21, John writes, *"And hereby we know that we are of the truth and shall assure our hearts before Him. (20) For if our heart condemn us, God is greater than our heart, and knoweth all things. (21) Beloved, if our heart condemn us not, then have we confidence toward God."* No matter how great my fears that God will be mad at me and not want to hear from me or on how far I think I've drifted, He absolutely is greater than all of my doubts, fears, anxieties, and sins—perceived or real! Hallelujah! Amen!! End of story. Let's Pray!

In effect, you will know you've gotten the most out of this book if you begin praying with joy. By using a few simple tools, not only can you begin to pray, but you can also begin to build your own prayers upon the principles, prompts and promises of God's word. This increases your joy and the joy of others.

CHAPTER ONE: First Things First

I'm going to call upon you to do two things as we begin to really dive into bringing life to your time in prayer. One is that you pray a simple prayer. In Luke Chapter Eleven, one of Jesus disciples (I'm glad we don't know their name—they all needed prayer just like us!) asked Him, "Lord, teach us to pray..." If Jesus' earliest disciples needed help, and they asked and got what they needed, why not us? So, pray that prayer right now.

"Lord, teach me to pray. In Jesus' name, Amen." To be clear: you need to pray that as an act of faith. Believe that! As we talk about prayer, the very Holy Spirit of God is doing His work to guide you, teach you, urge you and reward you in prayer.

Now the second thing I'm going to ask you to do is to use a simple acrostic to prompt your prayers: J-O-Y. That's it. The "J" stands for Jesus. We'll talk about the thoughts about God's greatness (who He is) and thank Him for His goodness (what He has done) and His gracious gifts and promises. The "O" stands for praying for Others. That's right. Praying for others before you pray for yourself will remind you that your focus should be on God and others before yourself. You may recall that in Jesus' instructions on prayer in Matthew 6:10, He had them pray "our Father..." not "my Father". We're in this together and we are built for and need one another. Out of humility, selflessness, and a servant's heart, our prayers will come to life. Finally, the "Y" stands for Yourself. God wants to hear your prayers, and He most definitely loves to answer them!

So, the way to use *Prayer Aflame* is to use a scripture starter from each category to ignite your prayers. Although it is fine to use a book which already contains prayers like a version of the *Common Book of Prayer* or Beth Moore's wonderful book *Praying God's Word Day by Day,* it would be my goal that you are able to compose and pray your own prayer from your own hand and your own heart. I really think that praying your own confident, heartfelt prayers to the Lord is what Jesus had in mind when He gave them the model prayer (See Matthew 6 and Luke 11).

How can something so sacred and supernatural be also simple and childlike? I recall a memory from my childhood when I was visiting my great grandparents. They lived way out in the mountains of West Virginia. You had to go off the interstate, state highway, two lane road, one lane road, gravel road, dirt road, one-lane wooden bridge and dirt road again to get to the old farmhouse where they lived. Whew! Makes me tired just thinking about how long it took to probably go not many miles back then. The journey caused almost a mystical thing to happen as we kind of went back in time with each mile to meet these magical people of a bygone era. One consistent thing was driving up to the old homeplace and seeing my great grandfather out in the front yard feed chickens with dogs running around. Just seeing him and hearing Grandad's car and him looking up to see us coming. His face would shine like the sun! Hear me well: although I stood in awe of my great grandfather, and I didn't even live in the old home place, I knew I was welcome there! He loved me like I was his own. After saying our "hellos" and entering the house, I'd sit at his feet and hear the stories and the wisdom roll from his lips like fresh honey. I was at home. I was at home in a place that was not my home. That, my friends, is what it is like to go before the God of heaven. To know that God looks forward to our coming, He delights in our presence. And somehow, we are all blessed by the time we share together. In a word...JOY!

CHAPTER TWO: Getting Started

An Awesome Truth

Before we jump into any more specifics, it is a good thing to slow down and be reminded of an awesome truth. God desires to meet with you. Yes! The Creator of the universe and Savior of your soul wants to meet with you. Scripture is full of verses expressing God's heart. He looks forward to an encounter with you on a regular basis. Now I've provided some verses here so you can be reminded of the certainty of this truth. As we begin the journey through this book, you may wish to dwell on one per day or read some or all of them as you start each day. It may also be helpful to read a single verse out loud or rewrite the verse in a journal. These actions link your human spirit's desire with the functions and thoughts of your body and brain, which will energize your time in prayer.

Henceforth I call you not servants; for the servant knoweth not what his lord doeth: but I have called you friends; for all things that I have heard of my Father I have made known unto you. John 15:15

Trust in him at all times; ye people, pour out your heart before him: God is a refuge for us. Selah. Psalm 62:8

If ye then, being evil, know how to give good gifts unto your children, how much more shall your Father which is in heaven give good things to them that ask him? Matthew 7:11

And whatsoever ye shall ask in my name, that will I do, that the Father may be glorified in the Son. John 14:13

But let him ask in faith, nothing wavering...Every good gift and every perfect gift is from above, and cometh down from the Father of lights, with whom is no variableness, neither shadow of turning. James 1:6; 17

The eyes of the LORD are upon the righteous, and his ears are open unto their cry. Psalm 34:15

For this shall every one that is godly pray...Thou art my hiding place thou shalt preserve me from trouble; thou shalt compass me about with songs of deliverance...I will instruct thee in the way which thou shalt go: I will guide thee with mine eye. Psalm 32:6-8

And ye shall seek me, and find me, when ye shall search for me with all your heart. Jeremiah 29:13

And in the morning, rising up a great while before day, he went out, and departed into a solitary place, and there prayed. Mark 1:35

And he spake a parable unto them to this end, that men ought always to pray, and not to faint. Luke 18:1

For this cause I bow my knees unto the Father of our Lord Jesus Christ...That he would grant you, according to the riches of his glory, to be strengthened with might by his Spirit in the inner man... Ephesians 3:14, 16

...and pray one for another, that ye may be healed. The effectual fervent prayer of a righteous man availeth much. James 5:16

Pray without ceasing. I Thessalonians 5:17

One glaring essential in jump-starting prayer is keeping it in its most simple and enjoyable form. II Corinthians 11:3 contains an encouraging phrase *"...the simplicity that is in Christ."* That should be a constant reminder not to let things like prayer become overly complex nor, on the other hand, rote. It's not that prayer should have no structure. But our body, mind, and spirit aren't trying so hard to keep a set of rules in prayer that we find it a tedious, dry task and not the deep, fulfilling wonder that it was meant to be.

So, let's consider a couple of things like time, place, and process for reigniting prayer. In I Thessalonians 5:17, Paul says, *"Pray without ceasing."* Paul certainly is not asking you to get on your knees and close your eyes while driving to work! So, what were his intentions? Paul is saying that prayer is possible at any time and in any place if we feel so led. To clarify further, prayer can be spoken out loud—but that is not always necessary or practical. Many prayers are recorded in the Bible, which means someone wrote them down instead of verbalizing them out loud.

I'm encouraged by what G. Campbell Morgan described in his commentary, *The Gospel of Luke,* when he described what prayer is: "It may be asked, How can people be always praying? The answer is that we must understand what prayer is. Prayer is far more than uttering words. I can pray when I do not think I am praying. We can pray without any words at all. Prayer, in the last analysis, is the urge of the life towards God, and spiritual things; the setting of the mind upon things above, as Paul has it. Every detail of every day can be mastered by that urge. Prayer literally means to wish forward. Prayer, then, is the desiring towards the ultimate, the urge that forever master life for the coming of the Kingdom of God, and the victory of all things spiritual. Now, said Jesus that, unless your life is of that nature, you will faint."

In Matthew 6:5-18, Jesus gives His take on the issue of prayer and fasting. In that passage, He makes it clear that God rewards prayer that is secret, not public. The truth is that many people don't pray because they feel self-conscious speaking out loud where someone might hear them and think they aren't using the right words. The Bible, through Paul, records that some prayers are so deep that our human spirit is not strong enough because of our infirmities so that the Holy Spirit intervenes with *"...groanings which cannot be uttered."* (Romans 8:26). If you live in a small home or apartment, it can be particularly difficult to make or find a prayer "closet." That again is part of why people give up on prayer as a regular, positive routine. So, allow yourself to let your prayers be short, or simply read scripture out loud, or even write your prayer thoughts down in a journal. God will honor your effort because of the step of faith that you are taking to connect with Him!

Now some people have no problem leading a public prayer—whether there are many people gathered, or just a few people in a small group of family or friends. Indeed, we see in scripture those very things, but we also don't *hear* the actual prayers of a lot of people in the Bible. It doesn't mean they didn't pray. It only means they weren't praying for publishing, which should be an encouragement for most of us. Prayer can take place at any time of the day, but getting alone with God early before the day gets busy or before you go to bed at night are good options.

The JOY Approach

AS TO FORM, I'D LIKE to suggest again a simple approach to start that you can expand as you go. But feel free to come back to this when prayer seems to become too rigid or complicated. Think of the word JOY. It is a biblical word that goes beyond momentary happiness. Happiness is a moment, but JOY lasts forever! So, I'd like you to consider praying through JOY. As I noted before, each letter stands for a key thought: J= Jesus, O= Others and Y= Yourself. Please note that when I say "Jesus" for the purpose of this acrostic, I am referring to anything related to the Trinity—be it the Father, the Son, or the Holy Spirit. For instance, Jesus made it clear that He and the Father are one (John 14:7-11).

First, start with a thought about the (1) greatness and awesomeness of God, and (2) the goodness of God. It can be hard to separate God's glory and goodness, but remember, Moses asked to see the glory of God, and God showed him "...*all my goodness...*" Either way, this focus on God first will encourage us and spark our hearts to believe good things can happen when we start to ask for His help. In Jesus' Model Prayer (also known as the Lord's Prayer) in Matthew 6, He had the disciples begin by "hallowing" God's name. That's adoration and praise of God's greatness and goodness, a good place to begin prayer. Then, as you continue in prayer, prepare to ask God by doing a heart check (more on this later in Chapter Three). Even though we don't have a specific "confession" part in the Model Prayer in Matthew 6, I think you will find that when you dwell on the greatness and goodness of God, you'll find yourself naturally taking time to confess. So, before you begin asking, take time to align your heart with

God's heart. Then, feel the great freedom to approach God for the needs and difficulties for others and yourself. Let that JOY—the joy of prayer—be yours!

CHAPTER THREE: Before You Pray

Imagine being asked to look over someone's printed report to make corrections and suggestions but there was no space that did not have writing on it. Difficult to impossible, right? Or imagine someone who has just come from a couple of power-packed high-tension meetings giving you five minutes before they go to some more back-to-back meetings. You are likely not going to have a great, meaningful, or effective conversation. You will feel rushed and anxious. It is important, if not essential, to practice clearing your body, mind and spirit before you go to prayer.

Silence/Quiet as a Spiritual Discipline

And when he had opened the seventh seal, there was silence in heaven about the space of half an hour. Revelation 8:1.

IMAGINE IT! SILENCE in heaven. No brush of angel's wings or singing, no instruments playing, no prayers being prayed. Not even God Himself speaking. Powerful. Valuable. Useful.

Many of us have been in an elevator, or in a group meeting or even visiting with a friend one on one and felt the awkwardness of silence. We may even have our "go-to" things to bring up to get the conversation started. For those who are more social, the idea of silence may be terrifying. Yet, imagine silence was not only a good thing but a rare spiritual discipline that can yield great benefits.

Let's examine this spiritual dynamic more closely by looking up the words for "silence" and "quiet" in the Bible using *Strong's Concordance*. For these examples, I am using the King James Bible indicated at the front of this book. If you do not have a *Strong's Concordance*, I recommend getting one. It is a great resource for gaining insight into the original words used in the scriptures.

- Old Testament (Hebrew word origins)
  - "Silent" or "Silence" (definitions from *Strong's Concordance,* mentioned above)
    - *Awlem* – to tie fast ("bind the tongue"). Psalm 31:18
    - *Duwmah* – to be dumb ("dumbfounded"). Psalm 94:17
    - *Duwmiyah* – to be still, silent, quiet. Psalm 39:2
    - *Damah* (primary root)– to be dumb, silent or fail, perish. Isaiah 15:1
    - *Demiy/domiy* (from *Damah*) - to cut off to be dumb, silent, etc. Isaiah 62:6
    - *Damam* (primary root) - to be silent by way of astonishment. Job 4:16
    - *Hacah/hasaw* - to hush, hold your peace (silent, still). Judges 3:19, Amos 8:3, Habakkuk 2:20
    - *Charash* (primary root) - to scratch, engrave, plough; to devise, as in secrecy hence to be silent or left alone, to be deaf. Isaiah 41:1, Psalm 32:3, Psalm 50: 3, 21
    - *Chashah* (primary root) - to hush, hold peace, silent, still. Ecclesiastes 3:7, Isaiah 65:6
  - "Quiet" (references that show examples)
    - If God can quiet the earth, He can quiet our body, mind, and spirit. Job 37:17
    - Quiet Leads to a relaxed spirit. Psalm 131:1-2
    - After times of disruption/war quiet is welcome. II Kings 11:20, Isaiah 14:7, Jeremiah 30:10
    - Quiet is aligned with wisdom. Ecclesiastes 9:17
    - Quiet is commanded. Isaiah 7:4
    - Quiet as part of the announced description of the righteous kingdom to come. Isaiah 32:18
    - Quiet as part of the ideal Christian life. I Thessalonians 4:9-12 (especially verse 11), I Timothy 2:2, II Thessalonians 3:12

- Quiet as an ornament that adorns a believer. I Peter 3:4, Proverbs 17:1, Ecclesiastes 4:6
- New Testament (Greek word origins)
  - "Silence," "Silent"
    - *Hesuchia* - stillness, desist from bustle or language. Acts 22:2; I Timothy 2:11-12
    - *Sigao* - to keep silent, to close. Acts 15:12; 21:40; ICorinthians 14:28 and 34; Revelations. 8:1.
    - *Phimoo* - to muzzle. Matthew 22:34; IPeter 2:15

Silence Used in a Negative Context

...the wicked shall be silent in darkness... I Samuel 2:9

- When enemies are silenced. Isaiah 15:1 (KJV)
- When silent, we give people the impression we agree with their sins by association. Psalm 50:21
- Silence of death. Psalm 94:17
- When David was silent about his sin with Bathsheba, he was affected spiritually and physically. Psalm 32:3
- Dumbfounded. Psalm 39:2
- Viewed as lazy, missing opportunity. Jeremiah 8:14 (translated "condemned" in HCSB)

Silence Used in a Positive Context

- Silence is a normal part of the believer's life and should not be feared. Ecclesiastes 3:7
- Silence can help you to avoid speaking at the wrong time. Amos 5:13, Psalm 39:1 (*I said, "I will take heed to my ways, that I sin not with my tongue: I will keep my mouth with a bridle, while the wicked is before me." (2) I was dumb with silence; I held my peace...*)
- Silence can help us experience the presence of God. Zechariah 2:10-13 (*Let all people be silent before the LORD, for He is coming from his holy dwelling...*) (See also Isaiah 41:1 for an example of the recognition of

God as God)

- Silence can help us as a pathway to repentance and revival. Lamentations 2:10 (*...the elders of Daughter of Zion sit on the ground in silence. They have thrown dust on their heads and put on sackcloth. The young women of Jerusalem have bowed their heads to the ground.*)

- Silence is, perhaps, the gateway to when our prayers are heard. Recall that Revelation 8:1 precedes 8:3 when the prayers of the saints are heard.

- Silence also offers the side benefit of removing clutter from the mind and increasing our focus. II 2Corinthians 10:3-5 (*...For the weapons of our warfare are not carnal, but mighty through God to the pulling down of strong holds; (5) Casting down imaginations* [reasonings], *and every high thing that exalteth itself against the knowledge of God and bringing into captivity every thought to the obedience of Christ."*

Developing Silence as A Spiritual Practice

ALTHOUGH SILENCE IS often linked to being quiet, meditation, or prayer it should be developed as a separate thing. Silence, unlike quiet, has the purpose of clearing things out. Meditation focuses on a spiritual truth to better understand and live it. Prayer may involve quiet, silence, and meditation as parts of a whole.

- Practice this both alone and in public settings. Perhaps this is best to start at home and then expand to going places and simply being silent. If you are with family or friends, you might want to let them know you will be practicing this discipline, or you (or they) might get frustrated. Remember: the goal of silence is just silence not necessarily to obtain something.

- Practice and increase slowly.

- Don't worry about trying to "achieve" something here. The benefits will not always be obvious at first. If you find that you want to nod off open your eyes and begin again.

- Designate specific times of the day, week, or special days (such as holidays) to be silent.

Starting with Confession

ANOTHER AREA THAT YOU may want to deal with before jumping into praying with the J.O.Y. method is confession. I'm not talking about going to a priest and trying to recount every little thing which you may or may not have done wrong. When we read, think, and pray about the greatness of God, it is natural to realize how *not* like God we are. Confession is a two-sided coin where one side is who God is (that's also adoration/appreciation) and the other side is who then we are *not* (which leads to humility). For example, "God you are relentlessly strong, and I am continuously weak." Some of our best prayers come from practicing humility.

Confession can also lead to repentance—not just when we have faltered due to human frailty and limitations—but also when we have sinned intentionally. Isaiah records in Chapter 59 and Verse 2 in the book of Isaiah that our "iniquities" can hinder our prayers. Confession can lead to good old-fashioned repentance and renewal (See II Corinthians 7:9-11).

Being in alignment with God gives us a sense of freedom that brings renewed joy in prayer. Recall a time as a child when you were sincerely saddened by something that you did that you knew was wrong. But remember how happy you were when you apologized and promised to do better? What a relief it was—and what joy it brought—when your parents or teacher forgave you and were no longer at odds with you! Closeness was restored and good feelings flowed once more. To be clear: God is not mad at us as much as He is mad at the costly effect of sin upon us and how that can cause us to live below the level of good and great things He desires for us. Better than the best of parents, He wants the very best for His children. Psalm 32 and Psalm 51 record David's heartfelt experience of getting himself back into alignment with God. The book of I Samuel records that David's adulterous affair with Bathsheba still resulted in the illegitimate child dying. However, David's relationship to the Lord was restored. After prayer, fasting and the sad passing of the child, David returned to regular worship (See II Samuel 12).

CHAPTER FOUR: As You Pray...An Example of "JOY"

At this point in the process, perhaps it would help if you could see what a J.O.Y. prayer looks like. Keep in mind that when you are learning a new way of doing something, it may seem awkward at first! But soon you'll feel the restful joy of connecting with our Lord!

Step One: J = Jesus (God's Greatness and His Goodness)

"GOD YOU ARE A STRONG Tower, my Rock, my protection (II Samuel 22:3). "You are strong when we are weak. Just as you gave Samson added strength to live and to do your will, you have shown yourself to be our strong protector. I'm thankful that you have shown your strength to others and to me."

Step Two: O = Others

"GOD, RIGHT NOW A FRIEND of mine is experiencing a lack of strength. They are weak, and it feels like their world is crashing in around them. They just don't feel they have the strength to carry the load. Lord, will you please be their Strong Tower. For your glory and their benefit, give them the strength to endure this time of weakness. Or, Lord, remove the stress that caused this problem."

Step Three: Y = Yourself

"GOD, MY LIFE RIGHT now is full of stress and anxiety within. I know I shouldn't worry, Lord, but I do. I face it, I admit it, I'm weak. As one person prayed, 'Lord, I believe. Help my unbelief.' Lord, may you grant me the strength of your peace to face these fears and watch you win over them despite my obvious weakness. Please do this Lord for your glory and for the benefit of me, your servant. In Jesus name, Amen."

KEEP IN MIND THAT YOU don't have to be as meticulous with each line of your prayer. That said, as you grow in your knowledge of God, be as specific as you can. For example, I can tell someone that they are important to me, but it means much more when I can tell them why they are important to me. Being more specific and detailed adds depth to our prayers and leads to greater joy and effectiveness.

CHAPTER FIVE: J is for Jesus – Prayer Thoughts and Praise for Who God Is

I magine you were meeting someone famous for the first time. You'd have in mind what words you would want to say, and you might even rehearse those words. If the person were some sort of royalty, you'd want to know their titles and something of their language. If you could have extended time and money, you might even bring a gift, a token, to show your high regard for the person you're going to meet. Oh, they don't need the words or gift, but it communicates your sincere thanks and the joy you're feeling while building good feelings between the both of you.

In this segment, I've provided some of my own thoughts about the greatness of God. My list could not possibly list all the greatness of our God. Feel free—-in fact I encourage you—-to add to the list as you read scripture and encounter God personally.

Each day, read through the list until a word, picture in your mind, thought, or feeling of awe captures your attention as to the greatness of God. Reread the verse out loud, even if only in a whisper. Take a moment and write the verse down. Because this is prompted by the workings of the Holy Spirit, please understand that you have just encountered God! Do this daily. Do not skip this step. It is the same as hoping for a fire and not lighting the match. You could get a fire, but it is rare and unlikely. Even if you go no further than this, you can still praise God. It can also be a starting point for the next several sessions of prayer.

Praise Starters

I will bless the LORD at all times; His praise shall continually be in my mouth. Psalm 34:1

- His Might and Majesty
  - *O LORD our Lord, how excellent is thy name in all the earth! Who hast set thy glory above the heavens.* Psalm 8:1
  - *If the foundations be destroyed, what can the righteous do? (4) The LORD is in His holy temple, the LORD's throne is in heaven: his eyes behold, his eyelids try the children of men.* Psalm 11:3-4
  - *For the LORD most high is terrible* [awesome/great]; *he is a great King over all the earth... (5) God is gone before us with a shout the Lord with the sound of a trumpet (6) Sing praises to God, sing praises unto our King sing praises. (7) For God is the King of all the earth: sing ye praises with understanding.* Psalm 47:2, 5-7
- His Omnipotence (All Powerful)

And I heard as it were the voice of a great multitude, and as the voice of many waters and as the voice of mighty thundering saying, Alleluia: for the Lord God omnipotent reigneth. Revelation 19:6

- His Worthiness

...I will sing to the LORD, for he hath triumphed gloriously (highly exalted)... (2) The LORD is my strength and my song; and he is become my salvation: he is my God, and I will prepare him an habitation (praise) Him; my father's God, and I will exalt him (3) The LORD is a man of war [warrior]; *The LORD* [Yahweh, I AM/ Covenant Name] *is the LORD is his name.* Exodus 15:1-3

- His Goodness
  - *Thou wilt shew me the path of life: in thy presence is fullness of joy; at thy right hand there are pleasures for evermore.* Psalm 16:11
  - *Every good gift and every perfect gift is from above, and cometh down from the Father of lights, with whom is no variableness, neither shadow of turning...* James 1:17

- ○ *The Lord is my shepherd I shall not want... (6) Surely goodness and mercy shall follow me all the days of my life: and I will dwell in the house of the LORD forever.* Psalm 23:1, 6
- ○ *O Lord my God, I cried unto thee, and thou hast healed me.* Psalm 30:2
- ○ *The LORD is my strength and song and is become my salvation.* Psalm 118:14
- ○ *...God is light, and in him is no darkness.* I John 1:5
- ○ *...if any man sin, we have an advocate with the Father Jesus Christ the righteous.* I John 2:1
- ○ *And he is the propitiation for our sins: and not for ours only but also for the sins of the whole world.* I John 2:2
- ○ *...I am with thee to deliver thee, saith the Lord.* Jeremiah 1:8

- His Patience and Power

The Lord is slow to anger, and great in power... Nahum 1:3

- His Consolation, Good Hope and Grace

Now our Lord Jesus Christ himself, and God, even our Father, which hath loved us, and hath given us everlasting consolation, and good hope through grace, (17) Comfort your hearts and stablish you in every good word and work. II Thessalonians 2:16-17

- He is the King Forever! (Sovereign, Commander in Chief of all, Benevolent Caretaker)

The Lord is king for ever and ever... Psalm 10:16

- He is the Fountain of Life
  - ○ *With Thee is the fountain of life: in thy light shall we see light.* Psalm 36:9
  - ○ *But whosoever drinketh of the water I shall give him shall never thirst; but the water that I shall give him shall be in him a well of water springing up into everlasting life.* John 4:14

- He is All Powerful

Ah, Lord God! behold, thou hast made the heaven and the earth by thy great power and stretched out arm, and there is nothing too hard for thee. Jeremiah 32:17

- He is Everlasting
  - ○ *...his ways are everlasting.* Habakkuk 3:6
  - ○ *Thus will I magnify myself, sanctify myself, and I will* [make myself] *known in the eyes* [sight] *of many nations; and they will know that I am the LORD.* Ezekiel 38:23
  - ○ *The LORD is my strength and my shield; my heart trusted in him, and I am helped: therefore, my heart greatly rejoiceth; and with my song will I praise him.* Psalm 28:
  - ○ *Now unto the King eternal, immortal, invisible, the only wise God, be honour and glory for ever and ever. Amen.* I Timothy 1:17
  - ○ *But thou art holy, Oh thou that inhabitest the praises of Israel.* Psalm 22:3
  - ○ *The LORD is my rock, and my fortress, and my deliverer; (3) The God of my rock; in him will I trust: he is my shield, and the horn of my salvation, my high tower, and my refuge, my savior; thou savest me from violence. (4) I will call on the LORD, who is worthy to be praised: so shall I be saved from mine enemies.* II Samuel 22:2-4
  - ○ *I will praise you, O lord, among the people; I will sing of you among the nations. (10) For thy mercy* [love] *is great unto the heavens, and thy truth* [reaches] *unto the clouds. (11) Be thou exalted, O God, above the heavens: let thy glory be above all the earth.* Psalm 57:9-11
  - ○ *Great is the Lord and greatly to be praised* [most worthy of praise]*; his greatness is unsearchable* [no one can fathom]. *One generation shall praise thy works to another, and shall declare your mighty acts. I will speak of the glorious honour* [splendor] *of thy majesty, and of thy wondrous works* [I will meditate].

Psalm 145:3-5

- *And I will pray the Father and he shall give you another Comforter, that he may abide with you for ever; (17) Even the Spirit of truth; whom the world cannot receive, because it seeth him not, neither knoweth him: but ye know him; for he dwelleth with you, and shall be in you. (18) I will not leave you comfortless: I will come to you.* John 14:16

- *Great is the LORD, and greatly to be praised in the city of our God, in the mountain of his holiness.* Psalm 48:1

- *For the LORD is good; his mercy is everlasting; and his truth endureth to all generations.* Psalm 100:1-5 (especially v.5)

- *I will bless the LORD at all times; his praise shall continually be in my mouth. (2) My soul shall make her boast in the LORD: the humble shall hear thereof, and be glad. (3) O magnify the LORD with me, and let us exalt his name together. (4) I sought the LORD, and he heard me, and delivered me from all my fears.* Psalm 34:1-4

You can also use the names of God to understand who He is and appreciate His greatness!

IN THE OLD TESTAMENT, names were created to apply to particular situations where God's greatness and goodness were exhibited. For example, Abraham calls a place "The Lord Will Provide" (*Jehovah-jireh*) because God provided a ram to take the place of Isaac as a sacrifice (Genesis 22:14). Thus, you can make your praise more personal as you come to encounter God in a more personal way. In the New Testament, the names of Jesus and the descriptions of the Holy Spirit give insight into the character and greatness of God. As you read, review, and record these verses and insights, add these beautiful names and descriptions to your songs of praise! As Richard Foster once said, "Real prayer comes not from gritting our teeth, but from falling in love."

CHAPTER SIX: J is for Jesus – Prayer Thoughts: Thank God for His Goodness

In contrast to prayer thoughts, we're looking to get ever more personal with God by offering up <u>loving expressions for what God has done</u>. The Bible is a document rich in recording people who expressed thanks to God for how they were positively blessed by God's activity in their lives. I can equate it to letting someone know how a gift or musical performance moved you or brought you a sense of joy. Often, it is the context of an exact moment when you feel like you need a lift, and someone sends you a card of encouragement. That card—which was only a couple of dollars at the store—is like gold to the soul, and you know that it came by the prompting of the Holy Spirit. It's the thrill of winning and feeling on top of the world. Getting your dream job or getting your degree from school. You could not have made it to the top without that person, song, note, or word. So often we read a verse or passage of scripture that matches what our soul is sensing and there is a resounding "Yes!" that wells up in us. This is the part of prayer where you realize those special spiritual moments where God is ever more real and personal. If recorded, like in a journal, these become a mountain of thanks upon which we can rely to build joy in good times and hope and peace in times of struggle.

Now I've listed some of my favorite verses that portray thanks. You can already guess how hard it is to narrow down thanks. In praising God's character and work, you have a single word with many facets. In giving thanks, you have many facets, but it can be hard to categorize them into a single word or adequate grouping of words. You can use my list to get you started. But I encourage you to add to the list as you are prompted. When you have settled on that special verse for the day, write it down and pray it aloud, if you like, to God. Be as specific as possible. "God, here is a verse that reminds me of a time when I was feeling low, but you gave me (strength, joy, peace, hope, money, patience, a friend, a word, a place to belong...)." Counting and recording these blessings will remind you that God is at work and desires an even deeper encounter with you.

Prayer Thanks

"I THANK YOU, GOD..."

- <u>Because You Are for Me</u>

...for God is for me. Psalm 56:9

- *For the eyes of the Lord run to and fro throughout the whole earth, to shew himself strong in the behalf of them whose heart is perfect (loyal) toward him...* II Chronicles 16:9
- *See, I have graven* [inscribed] *thee on the palms of my hands...* Isaiah 49:16
- *And Thou saidest, I will surely do thee good.* Genesis 32:12

- <u>Because I Am Your Creation.</u> *I will praise thee; for I am fearfully and wonderfully made: marvellous are thy works; and that my soul knoweth right well.* Psalm 139:14
- <u>Because You Chose Me.</u> *...I have chosen thee in the furnace of affliction.* Isaiah 48:10
- <u>Because You Gave Me Life Everlasting</u>
  - *But God commendeth his love toward us, in that, while we were yet sinners, Christ died for us.* Romans 5:8
  - *For by grace are you saved through faith and that not of yourself it is the gift of God. (9) Not of works lest any man should boast. (10) For we are his workmanship, created in Christ Jesus unto good works, which God hath ordained that we should walk in them."* Ephesians 2:8-10
- <u>Because You Let Me Partake of Your Nature.</u> *Whereby are given unto us exceeding great and precious promises: that by these ye might be partakers of the divine nature, having escaped the corruption that is in*

the world through lust. II Peter 1:4

- <u>Because You Are the Righteousness of God</u>. *For He hath made Him to be sin for us, who knew no sin; that we might be made the righteousness of God in Him.* II Corinthians 5:21
- <u>Because You Work in My Life</u>. *Being confident of this very thing, that he which hath begun a good work in you will perform it until the day of Jesus Christ.* Philippians 1:6
- <u>For All Spiritual Blessings</u>.
  - *I thank my God always on your behalf, for the grace of God which is given you by Jesus Christ; (5) That in every thing ye are enriched by him, in all utterance and in all knowledge; (6) Even as the testimony of Christ was confirmed in you: (7) So that ye come behind in no gift; waiting for the coming of our Lord Jesus Christ: (8) Who shall also confirm you unto the end, that ye may be blameless in the day of our Lord Jesus Christ. (9) God is faithful, by whom ye were called unto the fellowship of his Son Jesus Christ our Lord.* I Corinthians 1:4-9
  - *And of his fullness have all we received, and grace for grace.* John 1:16
  - *...present every man perfect in Christ Jesus.* Colossians 1:28
- <u>Because I Can Pray to You</u>. *...then began men to call upon the name of the Lord.* Genesis 4:26
- <u>Because You Are My Strength, Shield, and Song</u>
  - *The LORD is my strength* [of salvation] *and my shield; my heart trusted in him, and I am helped therefore my heart greatly rejoiceth; and with my song will I praise him...Save thy people, and bless thine inheritance: feed them also, and lift them up for ever.* Psalm 28:7-9
  - *For thou art my rock and my fortress; therefore, for thy name's sake lead me and guide me.* Psalm 31:3
  - *God is our refuge and strength, a very present help in trouble.* Psalm 46:1
- <u>Because of Gladness and Joy Forever</u>. *Therefore, my heart is glad, and my glory rejoiceth: my flesh also shall rest in hope. (10) For thou wilt not leave my soul in hell; neither wilt thou suffer thine Holy One to see*

corruption. (11) Thou wilt shew me the path of life: in thy presence is fullness of joy at thy right hand there are pleasures for evermore. Psalm 16:9-11

- Because of Freedom. *...If ye continue in my word, then are ye my disciples indeed: (32) And ye shall know the truth, and the truth shall set you free... (36) If the Son therefore shall make you free, ye shall be free indeed.* John 8:31, 32, and 36
- Because of Your Guidance and Plans. *For I know the plans that I have for you declares the Lord, plans for welfare and not for calamity to give you a future and a hope.* Jeremiah 29:11 (NASV)
- Because You Made Me A Child of God
  - *I write unto you, little children, because your sins are forgiven you for his name's sake.* I John 2:12
  - *The Spirit itself beareth witness with our spirit that we are the children of God.* Romans 8:16
- Because I Am a Joint Heir with Jesus. *And if children, then heirs, heirs of God, and joint heirs with Christ: if so be that we suffer with him, that we may be also glorified together.* Romans 8:17
- Because I Am a Partaker of the Divine Nature. *Whereby are given unto us exceeding great and precious promises: that by these ye might be partakers of the divine nature...* II Peter 1:4
- Because I Am a Warrior of the Most High God. *Thou therefore endure hardness, as a good soldier of Jesus Christ.* II Timothy 2:3
- Because I Have Your Continuous Presence
  - *And lo I am with you alway, even unto the end of the world.* Matthew 28:20
  - *The Lord is with you when you are with him. And if you seek him, he will let you find him.* II Chronicles 15:2 (NASV)
- Because of Your Blessings. *I will cause the shower to come down in his season; there shall be showers of blessing.* Ezekiel 34:26
- Because of Your Anointing/Unction. *But the anointing which ye have received of him abideth in you...the same anointing teacheth you of all things...ye shall aide in him.* I John 2:27
- That Jesus Prays for Us. *I pray for them. I do not pray for the world but for them which thou hast given me, for they are thine.* John 17:9

- <u>For a Clean Heart</u>. *For if our heart condemn us God is greater than our heart, and knoweth all things. (21) Beloved if our heart condemn us not, then have we confidence toward God.* I John 3:20-21
- <u>For Your Work of Righteousness</u>. *For He hath made Him to be sin for us, who knew no sin; that we might be made the righteousness of God in Him.* II Corinthians 5:21
- <u>For the Holy Spirit and His Working in Us</u>. *Now we have received...the spirit which is of God; that we might know the things that are freely given to us of God.* I Corinthians 2:12
- <u>For the Promise of Your Presence</u>
  - *...in my flesh I shall see God.* Job 19:26
  - *...I will never leave thee, nor forsake thee.* Hebrews 13:5
- <u>For Your Cleansing</u>. *I, even I, am he that blotteth out thy transgressions, and will no more remember thy sins.* Isaiah 43:25
- <u>Your Care</u>. *He shall feed his flock like a shepherd: he shall gather the lambs with his arm, and carry them in his bosom, and shall gently lead those that are with young.* Isaiah 40:11
- <u>For Your Gentleness</u>. *...thy gentleness hath made me great.* Psalm 18:35
- <u>You Have Made Us Incorruptible</u>. *Being born again, not of corruptible seed, but of incorruptible,* I Peter 1:23
- <u>That You are the Cure for Wanting</u>. *Thou art my portion, O Lord...* Psalm 119:57
- <u>For Clearing My Record</u>. *....all that believe are justified from all things,* Acts 13:39
- <u>You Are Always Listening</u>. *Blessed be God, which hath not turned away my prayer,* Psalm 66:20
- <u>You Are My Strength</u>. *...the people that do know their God shall be strong,* Daniel 11:32
- <u>Your Leadership</u>.
  - *And He led them forth by the right way,* Psalm 107:7
  - *And the Lord sent before them by day in a pillar of a cloud, to lead them in the way; and by night in a pillar of fire, to give light; to go by day and night:* Exodus 13:21
  - *For it is God which worketh in you both to will and to do of his good pleasure.* Philippians 2:13

- <u>You Supply All I Need</u>. *But my God shall supply all your need according to his riches in glory by Christ Jesus.* Philippians 4:19
- <u>You Are My True Inheritance</u>. *The LORD is the portion of my inheritance and of my cup: Thou dost maintainest my lot. The* [boundary] *lines are fallen unto me in pleasant places; yea I have a goodly heritage.* Psalm 16:5-6
- <u>For Glorifying Me</u>. *...whom He justified, them He also glorified.* Romans 8:30
- <u>You Forgive and Forget My Sin</u>.
    - *If thou, LORD, shouldest mark iniquities, O Lord, who shall stand? But there is forgiveness with thee, that thou mayest be feared.* Psalm 130:3-4
    - *...their sins and their lawless deeds I will remember no more.* Hebrews 10:17
- <u>For Your Sovereign Power (All Knowing, Perfect Ruler)</u>. *And I will deliver thee out of the hand of the wicked, and I will redeem thee out of the hand of the terrible.* Jeremiah 15:21
- <u>For Your Joy</u>. *....I will rejoice over them to do them good,* Jeremiah 32:41
- <u>For Removing My Sins</u>. *As far as the east is from the west, so far hath He removed our transgressions from us.* Psalm 103:12
- <u>For Your Abiding Presence</u>. *...and lo, I am with you alway, even unto the end of the world.* Matthew 28:20
- <u>Because You Are My Shepherd</u>.
    - *He shall feed his flock like a shepherd: He shall gather the lambs with His arm, and carry them in his bosom, land shall gently lead those that are with young.* Isaiah 40:11
    - *The LORD is my shepherd; I shall not want.* Psalm 23:1
- <u>For the Promise of Strength</u>. *...I will strengthen thee; yea, I will help thee; yea I will uphold thee with the right hand of my righteousness.* Isaiah 41:10
- <u>For Your Protection</u>. *The LORD is my rock, and my fortress, and my deliverer; My God, my strength, in whom I will trust; My buckler* [shield] *and the horn of my salvation, my high tower* [stronghold]. Psalm 18:2
- <u>There Is Now No Condemnation</u>. *There is therefore now no*

condemnation to those who are in Christ Jesus, who walk after [according] *to the flesh, but according to the Spirit.* Romans 8:1

- You Overcome Our Lack of Peace, Tribulation, and the World. *These things I have spoken unto you, that in Me ye might have peace. In the world you shall have tribulation: but be of good cheer; I have overcome the world. John 16:33*

- You Made Me More Than a Conqueror. *...in all these things we are more than conquerors through Him that loved us.* Romans 8:37

- You Plead My Cause. *O Lord, Thou hast pleaded the causes of my soul; Thou hast redeemed my life.* Lamentations 3:58

- You Are Forever With Me. *...God is with us.* Isaiah 8:10

- You Are My Refuge. *The Lord of hosts is with us; The God of Jacob is our refuge. Selah.* Psalm 46:7

- Our Destiny Is in His Capable Hands. *But as for you, go on your way to the end; you will rest, then rise to your destiny at the end of the days.* Daniel 12:13 (HCSB)

- You Refresh Me. *And the parched ground shall become a pool.* Isaiah 35:7

- You Have Me on Your Mind. *What is man, that thou art mindful of him? And the son of man, that thou visitest him? (5) For thou has made him a little lower than the angels, and hast crowned him with glory and honour.* Psalm 8:4-5

- You Never Forget Me. *Thus saith the LORD; I remember thee, the kindness of thy youth, the love of thine espousals, when thou wentest after me in the wilderness, in a land that was not sown.* Jeremiah 2:2

- You Will Help Me. *For I the Lord thy God will hold thy right hand, saying unto thee, Fear not; I will help thee.* Isaiah 41:13

- You Delight in My Prayer. *...the prayer of the upright is his delight.* Proverbs 15:8

- Your Mercy Never Cease. *Blessed be God, which hath not turned away my prayer, nor his mercy from me.* Psalms 66:20

- You Approve of Me Enjoying Success from My Labors. *Behold that which I have seen: it is good and comely for one to eat and to drink, and to enjoy the good of all his labor that he taketh under the sun all the days of his life, which God giveth him; for it is his portion.* Ecclesiastes 5:18

- <u>I am on Your Mind- You Never Forget Me</u>. *I remember thee...* Jeremiah 2:2
- <u>Heaven Awaits</u>. *Let not your heart be troubled: ye believe in God, believe also in me. (2) In my Father's house are many mansions: if it were not so, I would have told you. I go to prepare a place for you. (3) And if I go and prepare a place for you I will come again, and receive you unto myself; that where I am, there ye may be also.* John 14:1-3
- <u>For the Crown to Come</u>. *Henceforth there is laid up for me a crown of righteousness, which the Lord, the righteous judge, shall give me at that day; and not to me only, but unto all them that love his appearing.* 2 Timothy 4:8

CHAPTER SEVEN: Thorns and Thistles: Praying for Others and Yourself

A thistle is a prickly plant with a purple flower. When we are asking God for something for others or for ourselves, we may find that it is because they or we have become entangled by something that looks good on the outside but can choke us or sting us when we get involved with it. In addition, a thorn may be something which gives us pain now and perhaps even an ongoing hurt that we will keep on having trouble dealing with.

The needs we pray for may be in areas spiritual, mental, physical, social, or emotional. Promises abound in scripture for all these items that we can bring to God for help. But there is a word of caution. Our goal is His will be done on earth as it is in heaven—not *our* will be done as it is for my personal ease, comfort, and pleasure. Now, God does, at times, give us the desires of our heart. This is especially true when our mission, goals and daily actions align with His mission, goals, and daily actions. So, as we enter this action of prayer, it is important to ensure our heart's desires align with His before we ask for anything.

As you read each scripture, review your attitudes and actions, repent (which means to change course/dedicate to be more like Christ in attitude and action), revive (let the Holy Spirit restore your inner peace and joy, see Psalm 51), restore (your relationship to the Lord, yourself, accepting that none of us is perfect), and repair any relationships that come to mind (in your heart is fine if talking to the person is not possible).

Let's look at some key scriptures that will prompt us to think about asking for God's helping hand in the lives of others and ourselves.

Key Scriptures

USING THESE VERSES, and the ones He calls to your mind, begin praying for others by being as scriptural and specific as possible.

- Take Charge of Your Soul. *In your patience possess ye your souls.* Luke 21:19
- Start with God's Word. *Sanctify them through thy truth: thy word is truth.* John 17:17
- Ask God to Reveal Any Hindrance. *...shew me wherefore thou contendest with me.* Job 10:2
- Ensure A Proper Attitude. *...before honor comes humility.* Proverbs 18:12
- Yield to Him. *I Beseech you therefore, brethren by the mercies of God, that you present your bodies a living sacrifice, holy, acceptable to God which is your reasonable service. (2) And do not be conformed to this world, but be transformed by the renewing of your mind, that you may prove what is that good, and acceptable, and perfect will of God.* Romans 12:1-2
- Learn from Him. *Shew me thy ways, O LORD; Teach me thy paths. (5) Lead me in thy truth and teach me: for thou art the God of my salvation; on thee do I wait all the day.* Psalm 25:4-5
- Cultivate A Passion for Purity and Its Blessings. *Therefore dear friends, since we have such promises, we should wash ourselves clean from every impurity of the flesh and spirit, making our sanctification complete in the fear of God... Now I am rejoicing, not because you were grieved, but because your grief led to repentance. For you were grieved as God willed, so that you didn't experience any loss from us. For godly grief produces a repentance to be regretted and leading to salvation, but worldly grief produces death. For consider how much diligence this very thing—this grieving as God wills—has produced in you: what a desire to clear yourselves, what indignation. What fear, what deep longing, what zeal, what justice! In every way you have commended yourselves to be pure in*

this matter. II Corinthians 7:1, 9-11 (HCSB)

- <u>Choose to Believe That—Whatever the Result of Your Prayer—It
Will Be Right for All Concerned</u>.
    - *And we know that all things work together for good to them that
    love God, to them who are the called according to His purpose.*
    Romans 8:28
    - *Rejoice in the Lord always; again I will say, rejoice!* Philippians
    4:1

CHAPTER EIGHT: O is for Others – Intercession

Rejoice with those who rejoice, and weep with those who weep. Romans 12:15

- <u>Praying for the Weak</u>. *We then that are strong ought to bear the infirmities of the weak, and not to please ourselves.* Romans 15:1
- <u>Family</u>. *And when Jesus was come into Peter's house, he saw his wife's mother laid, and sick of a fever. (15) And he touched her hand, and the fever left her: and she arose, and ministered unto them.* Matthew 8:14-15
- <u>Friends</u>.
    - *A friend loveth at all times, and a brother is born for adversity.* Proverbs 17:17
    - *A man that hath friends must shew himself friendly: and there is a friend that sticketh closer than a brother.* Proverbs 18:24
    - *After Job had prayed for his friends, the LORD restored his prosperity and doubled his previous possessions.* Job 42:10 (HCSB)
    - *... a servant of Christ, saluteth you, always laboring fervently for you in prayers, that ye may stand perfect and complete in all the will of God.* Colossians 4:12
    - *Bear ye one another's burdens, and so fulfill the law of Christ.* Galatians 6:2
    - *Therefore his sisters sent unto him, saying, Lord, behold, he whom thou lovest is sick.(4) When Jesus heard that he said, This sickness is not unto death, but for the glory of God, that the Son of God might be glorified thereby.* John 11:3-4

- <u>Neighbors</u>. ...*thou shalt love thy neighbor as thyself: I am the LORD* Leviticus 19:18
- <u>Foes</u>.
    - *But I say unto you, Love your enemies, bless them that curse you, do good to them that hate you, and pray for them which despitefully use you and persecute you...* Matthew 5:44
    - *If it be possible, as much as lieth in you, live peaceably with all men...(19)... avenge not yourselves...(20) Therefore if thine enemy hunger, feed him; if he thirst, give him drink: for in so doing thou shalt heap coals of fire on his head. Be not overcome of evil but overcome evil with good.* Romans 12:18-21
- <u>Church and Partner/Members</u>.
    - *As we have therefore opportunity, let us do good unto all men, especially unto them who are of the household of faith.* Galatians 6:10
    - *For this cause I bow my knees unto the Father of our Lord Jesus Christ, (15) Of whom the whole family in heaven and earth is named, (16)That he would grant you, according to the riches of his glory, to be strengthened with might by his Spirit in the inner man; (17) That Christ may dwell in our hearts by faith that ye being rooted and grounded in love, (18)May be able to comprehend with all saints what is the breadth, and length, and depth, and height; (19) And to know the love of Christ, which passeth knowledge, that ye might be filled with all the fullness of God. (20) Now unto him that is able to do exceeding abundantly above all that we ask or think, according to the power that worketh in us, (21) Unto him be glory in the church by Christ Jesus throughout all ages, world without end. Amen.* Ephesians 3:14-21
    - *I pray for them: I pray not for the world, but for them which thou hast given me; for they are thine. (10) And all mine are thine, and thine are mine; and I am glorified in them. (11) And now I am no more in the world, but these are in the world, and I come to thee. Holy Father, keep through thine own name those whom thou hast given me, that they may be one, as we*

are. (12) While I was with them in the world, I kept them in thy name: those that thou gavest me I have kept, and none of them is lost, but the son of perdition; that the scripture might be fulfilled. (13) And now come I to thee; and these things I speak in the world that they might have my joy fulfilled in themselves. (14)I have given them thy word; and the world hath hated them, because they are not of the world, even as I am not of the world. (15) I pray not that thou shouldest take them out of the world, but that thou shouldest keep them from the evil (one). (16) They are not of the world, even as I am not of the world. (17) Sanctify them through thy truth: thy word is truth. (18) As thou hast sent me into the world, even so have I also sent them into the world. (19) And for their sakes I sanctify myself, that they also might be sanctified through the truth. (20) Neither pray I for these alone, but for them also which shall believe on me through their word; (21) That they all may be one; as thou, Father, art in me, and I in thee, that they also may be one in us; that the world may believe that thou hast sent me. (22) And the glory which thou gavest me I have given them; that they may be one, even as we are one: (23) I in them, and thou in me, that they may be made perfect in one; and that the world may know that thou hast sent me, and hast loved, as thou hast loved me. (24) Father, I will that they also, whom thou hast given me, be with me where I am; that they may behold my glory which thou hast given me: for thou lovedst me before the foundation of the world. (25) O righteous Father, the world hath not known thee: but I have known thee, and these have known that thou hast sent me. (26) And I have declared unto them thy name, and will declare it: that the love wherewith thou hast loved me may be in them, and I in them. John 17:9-26

- <u>Missions</u>. *Go ye therefore, and teach all nations, baptizing them in the name of the Father, and of the Son and of the Holy Ghost: (20) Teaching them to observe all things whatsoever I have commanded you: and, lo, I am with you alway, even unto the end of the world.* Matthew 28:19-20

- <u>Ministers and Ministries</u>.
  - ○ *Devote yourselves to prayer: stay alert in it with thanksgiving. At the same time, pray also for us that God may open a door to us for the message, to speak the mystery of the Messiah.* Colossians 4:2-3 (HCSB)
  - ○ *With every prayer and request, pray at all times in the Spirit and stay alert in this, with all perseverance and intercession for all the saints. Pray also for me, that the message may be given to me when I open my mouth to make known with boldness the mystery of the gospel. For that I am an ambassador in chains. Pray that I might be bold enough in Him to speak as I should.* Ephesians 6:18-19 (HCSB)

CHAPTER NINE: Y is for Yourself – Supplication

Praying for yourself is the last step in the JOY process. Do not miss out on this important part of praying! The pendulum of prayer can swing so far toward being other-focused that we fail to take the step of praying for our own needs. Like a good father, God wants to meet the needs and hear the joys of His children. Many of the things that we pray about for others we can also pray for ourselves. In fact, don't forget that Jesus in Matthew 6 gave the model or Lord's Prayer with the word "our" involved. Of course, we can pray for others and ourselves simultaneously. But there are also times when we need to talk to our Father about some very personal or special needs—and that is perfectly fine. So, be sure to look over the verses provided for "Others" and use these verses—along with your own collection of promises and principles based on the scriptures—to power up and finish up your prayers.

- The Armor of God. *(10) Finally, my brethren, be strong in the Lord, and in the power of his might. (11) Put on the whole armour of God, that ye may be able to stand against the wiles of the devil. (12) For we wrestle not against flesh and blood, but against principalities, against powers, against the rulers of the darkness of this world, against spiritual wickedness in high places. (13) Wherefore take unto you the whole armour of God that ye may be able to withstand in the evil day, and having done all, to stand. (14 Stand therefore, having your loins girt about with truth, and having the breastplate of righteousness; (15) And your feet shod with the preparation of the gospel of peace; (16) Above all, taking the shield of faith, wherewith ye shall be able to quench all the fiery darts of the wicked. (17) And take the helmet of salvation, and the sword of the Spirit, which is the word of God: prayer and supplication in the*

Spirit, and watching thereunto with all perseverance and supplication for all saints; (19) And for me, that utterance may be given to me, that I may open my mouth boldly, to make known the mystery of the gospel... Ephesians 6:10-19

- When Sin Is an Issue.

- *If we walk in the light, as he is in the light, we have fellowship with one another, and the blood of Jesus Christ, His Son, cleanseth* [purifies] *us from all sin.* I John 1:7

- *This is the will of God, even your sanctification...* I Thessalonians 4:3
- *And the very God of peace sanctify you wholly; and I pray God your whole spirit and soul and body be preserved blameless unto the coming of our Lord Jesus Christ. Faithful is he that calleth you, who also will do it.* I Thessalonians 5:23-24

- When Anxiety or Fear Is an Issue. *What time I am afraid, I will trust in thee.* Psalm 56:3
- When Things Are Tangled, and Many Are Offering Questionable Advice. *No man that warreth entangleth himself with the affairs of this life; that he may please him who hath chosen him to be a soldier. ... (16)...shun profane and vain babblings: for they will increase unto more ungodliness...(19)...depart from iniquity...(21) If a man therefore purge himself from these he shall be a vessel unto honour sanctified and meet(useful) for the masters' use, and prepared unto every good work."* II Timothy 2:4, 16, 19 and 21
- When Contentment Is a Problem. *But godliness with contentment is great gain. (7) For we brought nothing into this world, and it is certain we can carry nothing out. (8) And having food and raiment let us be therewith content.* I Timothy 6:6-8
- When Discouraged by Little or No Growth in Becoming Like Christ. *But we all, with open face beholding as in a glass the glory of the Lord, are changed into the same image from glory to glory, even as by the Spirit of the Lord.* II Corinthians 3:18
- When You Lack Patience and Impulse Is Rising. *Be still and know that*

I am God... Psalm 46:10. Note: For Moses, it was 40 years before he returned to Egypt to get God's people; For David, about 25 years pass between when he is anointed to be king and when he actually takes the throne over a united Israel; For Saul/Paul, it's about 14 years between when he is converted and rises to become the great missionary and writer of the vast majority of the New Testament.

- When Being Generous is Difficult. *Being enriched in every thing to all bountifulness, which causeth through us thanksgiving to God* [Or as some have translated it "You will be made rich in every way so that you can be generous on every occasion, and through us you generosity will result in thanksgiving to God."] II Corinthians 9:11

- When You Don't Have a Lot of Resources.
  - *A little that a righteous man hath is better than the riches of many wicked.* Psalm 37:16
  - *Let your conduct be without covetousness and be content with such things as you have. For He Himself has said, "I will never leave you nor forsake you."* Hebrews 13:5
  - *Better is little with the fear of the LORD than great treasure and trouble therewith.* Proverbs 15:16
  - *Better is an handful with quietness, than both the hands full with travail and vexation of spirit.* Ecclesiastes 4:6
  - *Grace be unto you, and peace, from God our Father, and from the Lord Jesus Christ. (4) I thank my God always on your behalf, for the grace of God which is given you by Jesus Christ; (5) That in everything ye are enriched by him* [see verse 4 Jesus], *in all utterance, and in all knowledge: (6) Even as the testimony of Christ was confirmed in you; (7) So that ye come behind in no gift; waiting for the coming of our Lord Jesus Christ: (8) Who shall also confirm you unto the end, that ye may be blameless in the day of our Lord Jesus Christ. (9) God is faithful, by whom ye were called unto the fellowship of his Son Jesus Christ our Lord.* I Corinthians 1:3-9

- When Success Seems Slow in Coming.
  - *But as for you, go on your way to the end; you will rest, then rise to your destiny at the end of the days.* Daniel 12:13 (HCSB)

- *Therefore, my beloved brethren, be ye steadfast, unmoveable, always abounding in the work of the Lord, forasmuch as ye know that your labor is not in vain in the Lord.* I Corinthians 15:58

- <u>When the Timing of Events Seems Off.</u> *But when it pleased God, who separated me... and called me by His grace...To reveal his Son in me, that I might preach him among the heathen; immediately I conferred not with flesh and blood.* Galatians 1:15-16

- <u>When Weariness Is an Issue.</u> *Come unto me, all ye that labor and are heavy laden, and I will give you rest.* Matthew 11:28

- <u>When Tempted to Not Give Your Best Effort.</u> *Whether therefore ye eat, or drink, or whatsoever ye do, do all to the glory of God.* I Corinthians 10:31

- <u>On Transformation of Thoughts</u>
  - *For though we walk in the flesh, we do not war after the flesh. For the weapons of our warfare are not carnal, but mighty through God to the pulling down of strong holds; Casting down imaginations, and every high thing that exalteth itself against the knowledge of God, and bringing into captivity every thought to the obedience of Christ...* II Corinthians 10:3-5
  - *And be not conformed to the world: but be ye transformed by the renewing of your mind, that ye may prove what is that good, and acceptable, and perfect, will of God.* Romans 12:2

- <u>When You Think That Others Are Supposed to Call and Care for You.</u> *He* [God] *shall feed his flock like a shepherd: he* [God] *shall gather the lambs with his arm, and carry them in his* [God] *bosom, and shall gently lead those that are with young.* Isaiah 40:11

- <u>When Family or Church Seems Too Scattered or Fragmented to Bring Back Together.</u> *And I will be found of you, saith the LORD: and I will turn away your captivity, and I will gather you from all the nations, and from all the places whither I have driven you, saith the LORD; and I will bring you again into the place whence I caused you to be carried away captive.* Jeremiah 29:14

- <u>When You Need to Be Fierce and Courageous.</u>
  - *...now the kingdom of heaven suffereth violence, and the violent*

take it by force. Matthew 11:12

- ○ *...be thou valiant for me, and fight the LORD's battles...* I Samuel 18:17

- When You Are Burdened about a Fellow Believer Who Is in Known Sin.

  - ○ *And this is the confidence we have in Him, that, if we ask any thing according to his will, he heareth us: (15) And if we know that he hear us, whatsoever we ask, we know that we have the petitions that we desired of him. (16) If any man see his brother sin a sin which is not unto death, he shall ask, and he shall give him life for them that sin not unto death. There is a sin unto death* [note—the sin of rejecting salvation through Christ]: *I do not say that he shall pray for it.* I John 5:14-16

  - ○ *Brethren, if a man be overtaken in a fault, ye which are spiritual, restore such a one in the spirit of meekness; considering thyself, lest thou also be tempted.* Galatians 6:1

- When Building Your Family, Business, or Church. *Except the LORD build the house, they labor in vain that build it: except the LORD keep* [watches] *the city, the watchman waketh* [stays alert] *but in vain.* Psalm 127:1

- When You Need to Pray for Those in Authority/Government. *I EXHORT therefore, that, first of all, supplications, prayers, intercessions, and giving of thanks, be made for all men; (2) For kings, and for all that are in authority, that we may lead a quiet and peaceable life in all godliness and honesty.(3) For this is good and acceptable in sight of God our Savior; (4) Who will have all men to be saved, and to come unto the knowledge of the truth.* I Timothy 2:1-4

- When Pain and Problems Are All Too Real, and You Don't Have Answers. *My brethren, count it all joy when ye fall into divers* [various] *temptations; (3) Knowing this, that the trying of your faith worketh patience. (4) But let patience have her perfect work, that ye may be perfect and entire, wanting nothing. (5) If any of you lack wisdom, let him ask of God, that to all men liberally, and upbraideth not; and it shall be given him.* James 1:2-4

- When You Are Unable, Too Feeble, or Too Injured to Get Things

<u>Done</u>.

- ○ *And lest I should be exalted above measure through the abundance of the revelations, there was given to me a thorn in the flesh, the messenger of Satan to buffet me, lest I should be exalted above measure. (8) For this thing I besought the Lord thrice, that it might depart from me. (9) And he said unto me, My grace is sufficient for thee: for my strength is made perfect in weakness. Most gladly therefore will I rather glory in my infirmities that the power of Christ may rest upon me. (10) Therefore, I take pleasure in infirmities in reproaches I, in necessities, in persecutions, in distresses for Christ' sake: for when I am weak, then am I strong.* II Corinthians 12:7-10

- ○ *... Not by might, nor by power, but by my spirit, saith the LORD of hosts.* Zechariah 4:6

CHAPTER TEN: The ACTS Approach

Another approach for keeping prayer on track is the acrostic ACTS: A=Adoration and Praise, C=Confession, T=Thanksgiving and S=Supplication (praying for yourself) and Intercession (praying for others). In many ways, this approach mirrors the teaching prayer of Jesus to his disciples in Matthew 6 often referred to the as "The Lord's Prayer". Although there is no specific mention of confession in the Lord's Prayer, I think that it can and should be a regular part of your prayer life. I think of confession as knowing who God is which leads to adoration, but this knowing leads us to the obvious fact that we are not Him! The first step of confession is recognizing who we are *not*. For example, if I confess/agree with God and say, "God you are holy." This also means that I can confess/agree with God and say, "God I am not holy." This leads me to ask and say, "God cleanse me and make me holy." You can see the natural progression of moving from adoration to confession, to asking, to being more confident in the fact of God filling you and using you for His glory and your benefit and to the benefit of others.

If you're familiar with the ACTS process, it's fine to use it as your process through prayer. But you may want to try the JOY approach just to be refreshed by something different. A great expansion of this concept of ACTS is found in "The 29/59 Plan" by author Peter Lord. This may be out of print so a used book may be the way to go.

CHAPTER ELEVEN: The Model Prayer

I appreciate the blunt way that John R. Rice addresses prayer in his book *Prayer: Asking and Receiving* when he says that prayer is just that: asking and receiving. That simplicity is what we are asking for! But I think that the Model Prayer (also known as the "Lord's Prayer") has some worthy bookends to be added. So, we'll take a brief look into the Model Prayer. I think that—to simplify it as much as possible—there are perhaps three main sections in this prayer. Adoration of God ("Hallowed be thy name"), Asking (for our needs), and Closing. Let's unpack these three areas briefly.

Adoration

OUR FATHER WHICH ART in heaven, Hallowed be thy name. The word "Hallowed" comes the Greek word *hagiazo* from the root *hagios* which refers to something "holy" in contrast to something common ("koinos"). An interesting use of the word is when it was applied to the gold laid over the Temple or the gift laid on the altar (see Mathew 23:17 and 19), ceremonial cleaning (Hebrew 9:13) and for the setting apart or aside for specific or special service (See Acts 20:32 and Acts 15:16). You can learn about these words and references through the *Strong's Concordance* and the *Vines Expository Dictionary of Biblical Words*. The idea that Jesus is projecting is that when we come to prayer, our first priority and concern is to acknowledge and applaud who God is. We enter into prayer by way of a reverent awe. We treat God's name with reverence and respect with the inner knowledge that we can also know that He is the most loving of Fathers (See Romans 8:15; Galatians 4:6 [Abba = is the difference between Father and Daddy]). Once again, this is sophisticated and reverent while being simple and relatable. Time spent in silence (to clear your heart and mind) and then in meditation (thinking deeply about how great God is) draws us to know that we can ask what we wish—not only because He can do it—but also to ask with reverence, and not demanding out of our selfishness.

Asking

- *Thy Kingdom come. Thy will be done in earth, as it is in heaven.* We may live on earth in a certain country, but as a believer we are of the kingdom of God and not Humankind. Daily we are asking God to help us navigate within the kingdom of Humankind by using and lifting up higher the kingdom of God. I think it is easy to imagine that in heaven when God says for everyone to do something there is no debate. We're asking for God to have His way in our heart and living practices and to also have His way when we are dealing with those in the kingdom of Humankind.

- *Give us this day our daily bread.* This does mean daily bread, but it also means so much more. It includes all the things that are the basic necessities of life. Of course, there are needs and there are wants! Sometimes the water gets muddied as to which is which. We need food, water, clothes and shelter to sustain us. We need a job or source of income to provide basic needs. Perhaps a way to get to work like a car or money for a bus. Basic needs yes. The nicest and latest cell phone? Perhaps not.

- *Forgive us our debts, as we forgive our debtors.* Debts can be financial, social (think owing a favor or an apology) and spiritual (the debt of love). Out of all the things mentioned in the Lord's Model Prayer, forgiveness gets special emphasis from Lord Jesus. In Matthew 6:14-15, Jesus added that our forgiveness is directly related to our ability to forgive others. In essence, if you refuse to forgive others, your forgiveness from God cannot occur. We see this further in Ephesians 4:32, which makes it clear that we must ourselves be ready to forgive as Christ forgave. No strings attached. Jesus didn't hold back any aspect of forgiveness. I sometimes encounter people who say, "I can forgive but I cannot forget." It's ludicrous to think that we won't remember when someone has deeply hurt us. That said, we can, over time and Christ's healing touch, begin to resume normal relationships with others. A person who does not forgive is chained to a subpar, ineffective Christian experience. You cannot worship, witness or work for the Lord effectively with an account of unforgiveness on the books. This bitter attitude is like taking a poison pill and then waiting for the other person to die. We get the true benefit when we by faith forgive even if we are not feeling it. (See Matthew 5:21-26; Matthew 18:15-35; I Corinthians 13; Proverbs 18:19)

- *And lead us not into temptation.* God allows many things. Within our Christian freedom, we can freely experience many things. But not all of them are beneficial and some of them are downright harmful (See ICorinthians 6:12)! If we prefer to avoid temptation, we are invited to pray and ask just that. For it to have its effect, we must believe that we don't need to go to that place, to have that item, to be with that person, or have that experience. Placing ourselves in the place of temptation is tempting God—and that is completely wrong. Our actions should be by faith. It's a recognition that—while something may be right or okay for someone else—you need God to remove that influence in your life to help you glorify Him and continue to be a blessing to others.

- *But deliver us from evil.* The Greek rendering here is an interesting one. It actually says, "deliver us from the evil one." That's right—you know who. The influences of the evil one are around us every day. Traps are set to render believers in general ineffective, but traps are also set sometimes with you specifically in mind. Never forget that we are in a battle. We are not on a playground, but a battlefield. Do you have a weakness and impulse for a certain thing which always seems to trip you up? A sin which easily besets you (Hebrews 12:1). We can ask and then believe that God will protect us (even from ourselves). Further, if we feel like the pressure is still there after praying for God to remove it from us, then here is where it gets interesting. If God does not remove the temptations and does not trap of the evil one, it means that God believes that we will recognize it and handle it or ignore it accordingly. The problem is not that God hasn't answered your prayer. It's that God is showing His confidence in you and your growth into the likeness of Jesus! Believe it!

Conclusion of the Prayer

THIS MODEL PRAYER CARRIES a conclusion. We started with adoration and praise and we somewhat conclude with it. Yet it is more. *For thine is the kingdom, and the power, and the glory, for ever. Amen.*

The conclusion is praise but it is also a confident recognition that all that we are asking and believing that we receive is hinged on the fact that it is His kingdom by His Power (*dunamis*- think dynamite- explosive power), for His glory and this has no ending!

The word "Amen" as widely known means "so be it" or "let it be so." This is affirmation
and fits together.

"Let what I have asked of Lord, be true. Let it be true in my heart. Let it be true in my daily things I deal with. Let it be true in your kingdom God on earth as it is in heaven. Let it be true Father for Your Glory and for the benefit of others. AMEN!"

CHAPTER TWELVE: Starter Prayers

This book is primarily about getting your prayer life back on track. My goal is to have you start praying on your own. In alignment with God's Word and by the true feelings of your heart, I believe you can pray effectively. Yet, if you are still frozen in getting momentum in your prayer life I've given a few starter prayers. These prayers are not magic. You must still align your heart and life to God and mean these from your heart for these prayers to have any effect. If you do use them, you may wish to rewrite them in your own words and even add scripture truths and promises to more personalize them. God bless you as you pray.

Emotional Strength

- J = "God, you are the God who heals (Isaiah 53:4-5). You are the God of peace (Judges 6:24). Jesus, you are our peace (Ephesians 2:14). Holy Spirit, you bring peace by the fruit of your abiding presence. God, I recognize that anything that derails that peace cannot harm me unless I give into it."
- O = "God, right now there is turmoil. We need your peace to rule in our hearts (Colossians 3:15). Fear and anxious thoughts have taken us captive, but we know that your perfect love casts out all fear (I John 4:18). Father, as you did for the disciples, help my friends and family to see Jesus in the midst of the storm and be comforted by His powerful presence. We believe, Lord, but help our timid unbelief in this chaos and uncertainty."
- Y = "Lord, the psalmist said, 'What time I am afraid I will trust in thee' (Psalm 56:3). Lord, calm my fears one by one as I think about

the things that are true, honest, just, pure, lovely and truly good. (Philippians 4:8). May the peace that I receive from you bring Glory to you and be a blessing to others. In Jesus name, Amen!"

Physical Strength

- J = "God, you are the Everlasting God. (Isaiah 40:28). You have no beginning and You have no end. I am in awe of that! You never sleep. You never slumber. (Psalm 121:3-4). In Your goodness, You are always watching with care over your people. I thank You for that."
- O = "Lord, I confess that we have become weary. We are tired, exhausted, in a word, spent. My friends and family can't go on—yet they must go on. They have to be responsible. Have energy and presence of mind to do their work. Lord, will you give to them of your everlasting strength. Give them energy and enthusiasm that can only come from you. Help them to rise up Oh, Lord."
- Y = "Lord I confess my own weakness. I've tried to hold all things together myself. I've tried to live a balanced life but all things around me have taken more than my body has to give. My strength is gone. My tank is empty. Oh, Lord I call upon you because you are the very source of my strength. You have everlasting energy. Give me the power of Your strength both to will and to do of your good pleasure. As things get done may you be glorified and may those around me be blessed. In Jesus Name, Amen.

Financial Strength

- J = "God, the earth is the Lord's and the fullness thereof; the world, and they that dwell therein. (Psalm 24:1). You provided for your people in the wilderness the daily bread of manna, and meat and water from the rock. Your goodness was given even with a grumbling group of believers. You amaze me Oh, God with your goodness!"
- O = "I confess right now, Lord, that we have not always been good at handling the resources you have already made available to us. We didn't always give you praise for the jobs we had or the roof over our

heads, the food we enjoyed or the clothes you provided. In fact, we often, in pride, took credit for your goodness. We didn't count our blessings. So right now, Lord, we realize that every good and perfect gift comes from you (James 1:17). Like sheep we have gone astray not realizing that you as the good shepherd have always guided us. Our friends and family need your provision Lord. We don't deserve it, but we ask by your gracious hand and your unfailing resources to provide daily bread."

- Y = "Lord, you are my shepherd and yet I find that my foolish heart wants. Lord, I place before you the very desires of my heart. Lord, I ask that if what I think I need is really just a want reveal that to my foolish heart. Lord, if what I want would be unhelpful remove my desire for it. What's more Lord, in those areas where I've presumed upon your goodness and overextended the reach of my finances give me wisdom and courage to pay these things back or sell them off with the joy of knowing that what you will put in its place will be far better. Let these things be Lord for your glory and for the benefit of those around me. In Jesus name, Amen."

Social/Relational Strength

- J = "Lord, you are the Lord who is ever present (Ezekiel 48:35). I can hardly imagine it! Amazing! We have no need to ever feel alone or abandoned because we have all we need in you. Jesus said, 'But I have called you friends' (John 17:21)."

- O = "I confess, Lord, that we feel like we have to have others and are often hurt or confused when things are not in harmony. We miss that closeness and companionship. Now, Lord, you are not a respecter of persons (Acts 10:34). You love people of all kinds and from all nations. In your Word, You interacted with many different kinds of people and even some who didn't understand you, lied to you, lied about you and even betrayed you when you were at your weakest moment. So, Lord, you know how it feels when you want to get along with others and still follow your word and your ways and find it difficult to get along. There were times when you had disagreements from long-time friends (John

11) and family (Matthew 12:46-50). It makes it tough, Lord, when we can't get along or even stay together. We ask for wisdom to know, speak and do the right things. And because we are not perfect and we know conflict, anger, disappointment and hurt can follow, help us to be able to do as you would do to dwell in true acceptance and harmony (Philippians 4:1-3). Help us to be one in heart even as you prayed. (John 17:21)."

- Y = "In my life, Lord, I ask that you cleanse my heart and make me an instrument of your peace (Phil. 4:1-3). Help me to do all I can do to bring about and experience a peaceful harmony with others (Romans 12:18). Give strength, even if it is just for a period of time or longer, that we must be separated. It will be tough, so I'll need your strength. Lord, your word says, 'There is a friend that sticketh closer than a brother'(Proverbs 18:24), and in John 15:15, you went so far as to call your disciples "friends". Unbelievable! I know that the one true friend I can count on and the only one I really need is you, Jesus! Help me as I seek to find all I need in you and rely less on others. Lord, I so want to glorify you in my relationships and to be of the greatest benefit to others. In Jesus name, Amen."

Mental Strength (Including Decision Making and God's Will)

- J = "Who can know the mind of the Lord? (Isaiah 40:13; Romans 11:34) God, you know all things. You are the Strong One who sees all things past, present and future (Genesis 16:13). My mind simply cannot wrap around that thought."
- O = "I confess, God, to sometimes thinking that I've got things figured out only to find that I'm an infant compared to what you know. God, you have knowledge, understanding and the wisdom to know how to apply both. (Proverbs 1:1-9) We don't have it except in pieces. So, for those who are my friends and family I pray that they will know your mind. The mind of Christ (Philippians 2). And that you would speak to their mind and their spirit to make the right

decisions. Good decisions go beyond just having information, Lord. Give us "unction" to move and to act by the Holy Spirit. Just as the kite is pulled by the wind, may the movement of the Holy Spirit draw us in the right direction."

- Y = "God, I ask for daily knowledge, understanding, wisdom and clarity of mind to do all the things which must be done. Quieten my mind to hear only your voice. Let not my spirit and emotions lose the steps or all the things that need to get done. And Lord, quieten the vain imaginations of my wandering mind and take every thought captive like a prisoner. Let me not give the evil one a foothold in my mind and then in my heart of emotions (II Corinthians 10). God, cast out every evil thought. I know I cannot keep every evil idea cast in front of me or control what others say but Lord, like David, I know you can cleanse and restore my mind and heart to be a clean Temple for you to dwell, feel at home in and be glorified by. Speak to my mind Lord your servant is listening. In Jesus name, Amen."

CLOSING THOUGHTS

SO, DID YOU PRAY? I'VE been on campouts where we wanted to start a fire. We might try for a while but not be serious if we were just on a day hike. If we were on an overnight campout, and conditions were ideal, we might be a bit more motivated out of wanting that feeling of success or just boredom. So, if the kindling was poor and there didn't seem to be much good ready wood or if it was taking too long, we knew that we'd be out of there the next day so no worries. In other cases, though, it would be super cold. Our bodies were shaking and there would be no warm food without it. Suddenly we were motivated. We'd scour the area for rocks to bank the fire, search high and low for kindling and wood and most of all we'd not give up until the fire not only started but it truly took off. Once we got it going everyone in the group would gather 'round, relax and work together to maintain the fire. That is how prayer is. How badly do you want or need prayer? I guarantee if the conditions are right, you will not rest until you are once again on praying ground, enjoying it, benefiting from it, and others around you will be drawn to do the same. So, as we close out our time together can I ask you to do one more thing? Let us pray! May God's richest blessings be yours as you journey with Him in prayer. Amen.

APPENDIX A: Old Testament Names of God

Names of God often describe the Essence of Who God is and can show the Expression of God's good and gracious acts. In effect, God does good things because of who He is. God IS great and God IS good. There are general names for God and then there are hyphenated or combination names of God.

General Names of God

- God: *El*
- God: *Elohim* (literally Gods, meaning an all-in-one God; see Genesis 17:1)
- Almighty: *Shaddai* (often combined with *El. El Shaddai* as in "God Almighty" or "Almighty God;" see Genesis 17:1)
- Lord: *Adonai* (Lord; if translated with capitals [LORD] it is likely *Jehovah* and not *Adonai*; see Isaiah 6)
- Jehovah: *YHWH* (Transliteration [taken from one language to another] from the Hebrew language to English. In Hebrew it is actually only 4 letters [*YHWH*]. It is likely that it has the meaning of "to be". When Moses asks, "whom shall I say sent me?" He is told to tell them "I am" has sent you. Jesus identifies with this name/title where he indicates "I am THAT I am;" see John 8:58. Other letters are added [*YaHWeH* = "Jehovah"] and then descriptors to make specific names like *Jehovah-Jireh*, "God Provides"; see Combination Names, below)

Combination Names

- God Provides: *Jehovah-Jireh* (literally "to see before" = He is in

process of providing even before I have or know about the need! See
Genesis 22:14)

- God Heals: *Jehovah-Rophe/Rapha* (to heal, restore, cure by God
  Himself; see Exodus 15:26)
- The Lord is My Banner: *Jehovah-Nissi* (literally "to glisten" =
  standard, memorial, banner, flag [our identity]; see Genesis 17:15)
- The Lord is My Sanctifier: *Jehovah-M'kaddesh/Maccaddeshcem*
  (literally the one who makes you holy or sets apart for divine use; see
  Leviticus 20:7)
- God of Peace: *Jehovah-Shalom* (the God who provides health, wealth,
  and wisdom; see Judges 6:24)
- God as Shepherd: *Jehovah-Rohi/Raah* (the one who guides, guards,
  grows, and leads to glory; see Psalm 23:1; Rev. 7:17)
- God of Righteousness/Justice: *Jehovah-Tsidkenu* (literally "stiff" or
  "straight"; never wavering, true; see Jeremiah 23:5-6)
- God Is There/Present: *Jehovah-Ahammah/Shammah* (continuous
  living presence; see Ezekiel 48:35)
- The Most High: *El Elyon* (see Isaiah 14:13-14)
- The Strong One Who Sees: *El Roi* (see Genesis 16:13)
- Everlasting God: *El Olam* (see Isaiah 40:28)
- The Lord of Hosts: or "Lord of the Armies;" *Jehovah Sabbaoth* (see I
  Samuel 1:3)
- The Lord God of Recompense: *Jehovah El Gmolah* (see Jeremiah
  51:56)
- The Lord that Smiteth: *Jehovah Nakeh* (see Ezekiel 7:9)

(SOURCES: *Ryrie Study Bible* by Charles Ryrie and *29/59 Plan* by Peter Lord)

APPENDIX B: Names and Titles of Jesus

At the name of Jesus every knee should bow, and every tongue confess that Jesus Christ is Lord. Philippians 2:10

Once again, this list is not exhaustive. Although there are many foreshadowing statements of Christ in the Old Testament, the New Testament is full of absolute statements. Feel free to continue to add to the list as you discover more names, ministries, and titles of Lord Jesus.

- Advocate. I John 2:1
- Alpha (Beginning). Revelation 1:8
- Anointed. Luke 4:18
- Brother. Matthew 12:50
- Carpenter. Mark 6:3
- Child. Matthew 1:21, Luke 2:27 and 40
- Chosen of God. Luke 23:35
- Christ. Matthew 16:16
- Comforter. John 14:16
- Commander. Matthew 26:53, see also "King of Kings"
- Cornerstone. Ephesians 2:20, I Corinthians 3:11, I Peter 2:7
- Defense (High Tower). Psalm 18:2
- Deliverer. Romans 11:26
- Door. John 10:7-9
- Emmanuel (God with Us). Matthew 1:23, Isaiah 7:14
- Eternal Life. I John 5:20
- Express Image of God. Hebrews 1:3
- Faithful and True. Revelation 19:11
- Finisher. Hebrews 12:2
- Friend. Matthew 11:19, John 15:14

- Gentle (Meek) and Lowly. Matthew 11:29
- God. John 1:1 and 14, Colossians 2:9
- Gracious. I Peter 2:3
- Harmless. Hebrews 7:26
- Harvester/ Reaper. Revelation 14:5
- Head of the Church. Matthew 16:18, Mark 11:15
- Healer. Mark 3:5
- Heir of ALL Things. Hebrews 1:2
- High Priest. Hebrews 3:1, 6:20
- Holy (and Just). Luke 4:34, Acts 3:14, Acts 4:27
- Hope. Acts 28:20
- House/Habitation/Shelter. Psalm 91:9
- Human (He could thirst, hunger, experience pain). Mark 8:31
- "I Am" (tied to Old Testament, The Covenant [promise], Exodus 3:14; name of God [*YHWH*= Yahweh= Jehovah =LORD (all cap when in an English translation)], John 8:58. It has the idea of I was, I am, I will always be; In other words, His words are true and truth and He can always be trusted [Immortal], I Timothy 1:17.
- Image of the Invisible God (Icon/ Picture of God in Person). John 14:9, Colossians 1:15, I Timothy 1:17
- Intercessor (He is ALWAYS praying for us!). Hebrews 7:25
- Jesus (From the Old Testament Hosea and Joshua meaning Salvation; *Yeshua*). Matthew 1:21
- Judge (Righteous Judge). Acts 10:42, II Timothy 4:8
- Just and Justifier. Matthew 27:19, Acts 3:14
- Keeper of the Keys of Death and Hell. Revelation 1:18, see also "King of Kings"
- King. Matthew 25:31, John 1:49, John 18:39; I Timothy 6:15, Matthew 12:42
- King of Kings. I Timothy 6:15 (also, Leader, Head of..., Colossians 2:10, Revelation 15:3)
- Lamb, Lamb of God. John 1:29, I Peter 1:19
- Law, Lawgiver. James 4:12
- Life. John 11:25, John 14:6, see also "Eternal Life"
- Light. John 1:4, John 1: 8-9, John 8:12, Luke 2:32

- Lion, Lion of Judah. Revelation 5:5
- Lord. Matthew 9:38, Matthew 12:8, Luke 2:11, Acts 7:59, Romans 10:12, I Corinthians 15:47, Galatians 1:3, Philippians 3:8, I Timothy 6:15, Revelation 15:3
- Man. John 19:5, I Timothy 2:5
- Master Craftsman (prepares heaven for us). Ephesians 2:10, John 14:2
- Master Fisherman. Matthew 4:19, Matthew 8:19, Mark 10:17
- Mediator. I Timothy 2:5
- Meek. Matthew 11:29
- Merciful. Hebrews 2:17
- Messiah. John 1:41
- Minister. Matthew 20:28, Hebrews 8:2
- Miracle Worker. John 2:11
- Morning Star (when things are dark). Revelation 22:16
- No Reputation. Philippians 2:7
- Obedient. Luke 2:51, Hebrews 5:8-9
- Omega (The End). Revelation 1:8,
- Omnipotent ("All Powerful"). Matthew 28:18
- Omnipresent ("Always Present"). Matthew 18:20
- Omniscient ("All Knowing"). John 16:30
- Overcomer. John 16:33
- Overseer/Director. John 21:15, see also "King of Kings"
- Owner (God) of the Earth. Isaiah 54:5
- Owner of All People. Psalm 24:1
- Owner of the Church. Matthew 16:18
- Passover. I Corinthians 5:7
- Peace. Ephesians 2:14
- Physician. Matthew 9:12
- Pierced. John 19:34 (He experienced and felt pain, He understands our pains)
- Poor (by the world standard). Luke 9:58 (our contentment is not based on the world's standards nor on the number of things we have nor status)
- Potter. Romans 9:21
- Power. John 1:12

- Preacher. Luke 4:18
- Prince of Kings. Revelation 1:5, see also "King of Kings"
- Prince of Life. Acts 3:15, Acts 5:31
- Prisoner. Matthew 27:15
- Prophet. John 7:40
- Purchaser. Acts 20:28
- Quencher. John 4:13-14
- Rabbi/Rabboni ("Teacher"). John 3:2, John 20:16
- Ransom. I John 2:6
- Reconciler. II Corinthians 5:19
- Redeemer. Galatians 3:13
- Reflection of the Father (for when God seems distant). John 14:9
- Resurrection. John 11:25
- Rewarder. Hebrews 11:6
- Righteous/Righteous Judge. II Timothy 4:8
- Righteous/Righteous Man. Luke 23:47
- Rock. Matthew 21:42, I Corinthians 10:4, I Peter 2:8
- Sacrifice. Ephesians 5:2
- Sanctifier. I Corinthians 1:30
- Savior (Hosanna). Mark 11:10, Luke 2:30, Acts 13:23, Titus 3:6 (literally, "Save now, please")
- Scholar. Matthew 7:29, Luke 2:46-47
- Servant. Matthew 12:18; as Foot Washer, John 13:5, Philippians 2:7
- Shepherd. John 10:11, I Peter 5:4
- Silent. Mark 15:5
- Sinless and Perfect. Hebrews 4:15
- Son of David (kingly lineage). Matthew 1:1
- Son of God. Matthew 17:5
- Son of Joseph (humanity). John 6:42
- Son of Man. John 6:27 (Jesus used this term more than any other about Himself).
- Son of Mary (miraculous birth). Matthew 1:1-8
- Substitute/Propitiation for our Sins. I John 2:2
- Teacher. John 3:2
- Tempted (yet without sin). Matthew 16:1, Hebrews 4:15

- <u>Truth</u>. John 14:6
- <u>Undeniably God</u>. Matthew 27:54, I John 5:20
- <u>Vine</u>. John 15:5
- <u>Warrior</u>. Matthew 10:34
- <u>Way</u> (<u>The Way</u>). John 1:6
- <u>Weeping</u>. Luke 19:41, John 11:35
- <u>Wisdom of God</u>. I Corinthians 1:24
- <u>Word of God</u> (*Logos*). John 1:1-2
- <u>Worthy</u>. Hebrews 3:3, Revelation 5:12
- X-factor (transfigured and able to transform). Matthew 17:2
- <u>Yokefellow</u>. Matthew 11:29-30
- <u>Zealous/Jealous</u>. John 2:16-17

APPENDIX C: Names, Titles and Ministries of the Holy Spirit

Neither will I hide my face any more from them: for I have poured out my Spirit upon the house of Israel, saith the lord God. Ezekiel 39:29

Another way to think of it is that to know the Holy Spirit in all His fullness is to see the face of God. The Holy Spirit is promised to all believers (Galatians 3:14). There are many names, titles, and expressions regarding the Holy Spirit. Some are included below.

Names and Titles

- The Holy Ghost. Luke 3:16, John 14:26
- The Holy Spirit. Isaiah 63:10-11
- The Spirit (His Spirit). Isaiah 48:16
- Spirit of the LORD. Judges 3:10, Isaiah 40:13
- The Spirit of the Lord God. Isaiah 61:1
- Spirit of Adoption. Romans 8:15
- Spirit of God. Genesis 1:1, II Chronicles 15:1
- Spirit of Grace. Hebrews 10:29
- Spirit of Revelation. John 16:13
- Spirit of Truth. John 14:17, John 15:26, John 16:13, I Corinthians 2:9
- Spirit of Wisdom (also understanding, counsel, might and knowledge). Isaiah 11:2
- The Comforter. John 14:26; II Corinthians 1:3-5

Expressions/Ministries

- He is the Advocate of the believer (*parakletos*, Greek). John 14:16 (Comforter, Helper, Advocate, Friend)
- He is the source of Assurance for the believer. I John 5:6-8
- He is the Anointing of the believer. I John 2:27
- He Comforts the believer. John 14:16, 26, John 16:7
- He Convinces, Convicts and (if belief occurs) Converts the unbeliever through the reality of sin, the truth about what is righteousness and of the judgement to come for those who do not turn to God. John 16: 7-11
- He is the Conscience to the believer and is the prompter to convict a believer who has wandered/drifted away. Psalm 139:7-24 (especially verses 23-24), Gal. 5:16-18
- He Conveys spiritual gifts upon the believer to build the body of Christ. Romans 12:1-10, I Corinthians 12:4-6, 8-10, 31, Ephesians 4:11-13, I Peter 4:8-11
- He Enacts the Plan of God. Genesis 1:1-2, Job 26:13, Hebrews 9:14
- He Engages the believer in the work of God by enlightening (enlisting, enabling, empowering, encouraging). Joel 2:28-32
- He Empowers the Believer in Service. Judges 14:6 (Samson) (Strength, Stamina, Courage...)
- He Exalts Christ. Matthew 4:16-17, I Corinthians 12:3
- He is Ever Present. Psalm 139:7-24
- He Guides. Acts 8:26, 29; 13:2-4
- He Manifests Himself or reveals Himself through a yielded believer. John 14:16-21
- He Seals the believer for eternity. Ephesians 1:13-14 (Also the idea of "guarantee")
- He Transforms the believer to experience and enjoy God's gifts and to become like Christ in the process. Romans 14:17-18

APPENDIX D: The Ten Commandments

You can pray through The Ten Commandments (found in Exodus 20:1-17 and Deuteronomy 5:6-21). In essence, they review our relationship to God and our relationship with others. A good simple way to think about life and keep our priorities right.

- *Thou shalt have no other gods before me.* Exodus 20:3
- *Thou shalt not make unto thee any graven image, or any likeness of any thing that is in heaven above, or that is in the earth beneath, or that is in the water under the earth: (5) Thou shalt not bow down thyself to them, nor serve them: for I the LORD thy God am a jealous God, visiting the iniquity of the fathers upon the children unto the third and fourth generation of them that hate me; (6) And shewing mercy unto thousands of them that love me and keep my commandments.* Exodus 20:4-6
- *Thou shalt not take the name of the LORD thy God in vain; for the LORD will not hold him guiltless that taketh his name in vain.* Exodus 20:7
- *Remember the Sabbath day, to keep it holy. (9) Six days shalt thou labour, and do all they work: (10) But the seventh day is the Sabbath of the LORD thy God: in it thou shalt not do any work, thou, nor they son, nor they daughter, thy manservant, nor they maidservant, nor they cattle, nor they stranger that is within thy gates: (11) For in six days the LORD made heaven and earth, the sea and all that in them is, nd rested the seventh day: wherefore the LORD blessed the Sabbath day and hallowed it.* Exodus 20:8-11
- *Honour they father and thy mother: that they days may be long upon the land which the LORD thy God giveth thee.* Exodus 20:12
- *Thou shalt not kill.* Exodus 20:13
- *Thou shalt not commit adultery.* Exodus 20:14

- *Thou shalt not steal.* Exodus 20:15
- *Thou shalt not bear false witness against thy neighbor.* Exodus 20:16
- *Thou shalt not covet they neighbour's house, thou shalt not covet thy neighbour's wife, nor his manservant, nor his maidservant, nor his ox, nor his ass, nor any thing that is thy neighbour's.* Exodus 20:17

APPENDIX E: Prayer and Fasting

Prayer and Fasting are often listed together in scripture. There are times and circumstances which may call for a more intensified type of praying which can come about through fasting (see Matthew 17:14-21). The idea is that you are giving up something and in place of that thing you devote the time to prayer. You may need to consult a physician and let at least one family member or close friend know you are fasting (if you are fasting from food) just in case there is a medical situation that arises from fasting.

The tradition of fasting usually includes not eating for a set time, and there are people who fast as a way of life. This could be a single day or several days. A person could abstain from one meal each week and devote that time to reading scripture or praying. In addition, those who cannot abstain from food could abstain from something else. Taking a break from your phone, social media, favorite sport, etc., and devoting that time to undistracted, concentrated reading of the Bible or praying can help focus your attention on specific issues. Reading about times in scripture that people have fasted may give insight into what type of fast you need to pursue—and if you need to enter a season of fasting.

The Bible says in Matthew 6:16-18 that you should not draw attention to yourself when you are fasting: *Moreover, when ye fast, be not, as the hypocrites, of a sad countenance: for they disfigure their faces, that they may appear unto men to fast. Verily I say unto you, They have their reward. (17) But thou, when thou fastest, anoint thine head, and wash thy face: (18) That thou appear not unto men to fast, but unto thy Father, which seeth in secret, shall reward thee openly.*

Fasting through the Scripture

- In a time of civil Unrest; Declining Morality, Civil Division. Judges 19-21 (especially 20:26-28).

- Rededication and Advent of War. I Samuel 7:1-13 (especially verse 6).
- Fallout of Sin, Sickness of a Child. I Samuel 12:1-25 (especially verses 15-24).
- Misuse of a Fast for personal gain. I Kings 21:1-29.
- Upon the death of a leader. I Chronicles 10:1-14 (especially verses 11-12).
- National Crisis; Advent of War. II Chronicles 20:1-4.
- Direction of a group, children, and protection of belongings. Ezra 8:21-23.
- When a nation/organization/church has fallen or is under threat. Nehemiah 1:1-11 (especially verses 4-11).
- Rededication. Nehemiah 9:1-3.
- Religious Persecution. Esther 4:1-17 (see verses 3 and 16).
- To Commemorate/Celebrate Past Victories. Esther 9:31.
- When facing opposition. Psalm 35:13.
- When feeling down, overwhelmed and weak. Psalm 69:1.
- When others are lying and are against you. Psalm 109:24.
- When renewal is desperately needed. Isaiah 58:1-59:4 (especially 58:3-12).
- When a breakthrough is needed but clouded by sin and powerless Religion. Jeremiah 14:7-13.
- Combined with the public reading of God's word. Jeremiah 36:5-10.
- When you are uncertain about decisions you've already made. Daniel 6:18-23.
- When burdened to pray for a group's renewal (For example a nation, church, family or organization). Daniel 9:1-22 (see verse 3).
- Part of the steps of Revival and Spiritual Awakening. Joel 1:14; 2:12-17.
- National Fast for Spiritual Awakening. Jonah 3:5.
- False Fasting and Authentic fasting contrasted. Zechariah 7:1-8:21 (See 7:5-6; 8:19-21).
- Temptation of Jesus. Matthew 4:2.
- Teaching on Fasting (being quiet about it avoids pride). Matthew 6:16-18.
- Teaching on prayer, fasting and healing. Matthew 9:14-29; (Mark

2:18-22; Luke 5:33-35).

- Prayer and Fasting as a regular ministry. Luke 2:37.
- Teaching about true prayer and fasting. Luke 18:9-14.
- Spiritual hunger that leads to salvation. Acts 10:30.
- Decision Making. Acts 13:2-3.
- Appointing and developing leaders. Acts 14:23.
- Fasting as a part of ongoing spiritual disciplines. Acts 27:9 (See Leviticus 16:29-34).
- As a regular part of ministry. II Corinthians 6:1-10 (especially v.5); 11:22-31 (especially v.27).

APPENDIX F: Example Prayers in Scripture

Any person speaking with God in the Bible could be considered prayer. This is the reason, perhaps, why lists of prayers in the Bible vary from writer to writer. Likewise, many of the psalms are written but obviously were songs that at one time were sung and were in many cases a type of prayer. This list is helpful if you are just looking to hear other people at prayer to prompt you to see a connection that you identify with then spur prayer in your own life.

- The Birth of Prayer. Genesis 4:26
- Following God's Will. Genesis 12
- Covenant. Genesis 17
- Even for One. Genesis 18:23
- Prayers in Harm's Way. Exodus 3 and following (Moses and God talk many times; Numbers 11:1-3)
- The One-Sided Prayer. Numbers 6:2-27
- Praying for the Opposition. Numbers 12:1-16 (See Numbers 14, 15, 16, 21)
- Living Beyond Jordan. Deuteronomy 3:23-25
- Praying in the Gap. Deuteronomy 9:20, 26-29
- Praying in Defeat. Joshua 7:6-9
- Praying for God's Help/Will. Judges 1:1-4, 6:12-14, 36-40
- Prayer Bargains. Judges 10, 11:30-31, 16:28-31 (Samson)
- God Bless You. Ruth 1:8-9, 2:4, 2:12, 4:11, 4: 14-15 (Greetings, Partings as Prayer)
- Prayers of the Heart. I Samuel 1:9-13 (Read with Romans 8:22-28)
- Prayers in Times of Change. I Samuel 3, 8:6, 12:18, 14:35, 15:11, 16:1-12
- When God Says No. II Samuel 12:16 (Read with II Corinthians 12:7-10)

- Famine in the Soul. II Samuel 21:1-12
- Before the Altar of God. I Kings 8:12-61 (Read with II Chronicles 7:14)
- Open My Eyes Lord. II Kings 6:17
- Death Prayer. II Kings 20:1-3 (See also II Kings 19:15-19)
- Prayer for Prosperity. I Chronicles 4:9-10 (See also Luke 22:31-32)
- Rest on Thee. II Chronicles 14:11 and 15:10-15
- Blessed be the Name. Ezra 7:27-28, 8:21-23, 9:5-10:4
- Nevertheless. Nehemiah 4:7-9 (See also 1:4-11, 2:4-5)
- Prayers of A Wounded Heart. Job 1:20-22, 6:8-9, 38, 40 (Much of the book is Job talking to God)
- Prayer for My Friends. Job 42:7-10
- Not of Ten Thousand. Psalm 3
- At The Cross. Psalm 22
- Even the Greatest Sin. Psalm 32 and 51
- The Patient Prayer. Psalm 40
- Any Wicked Way in Me. Psalm 139
- Here Am I. Isaiah 6:1-13 (See also I Samuel 23:2, 10-12)
- The Scuttled Prayer. Lamentations 3:8, 37-66
- Upon My Face. Ezekiel 9:8, 11:3-16
- Three Times a Day. Daniel 2:16-23, 6:10-15, 9:4-19, 10:4-27
- The Reluctant Prayer. Jonah (The book is a continuous dialogue between God and Jonah)
- The Prayer of Revival. Habakkuk 3:1-19
- A Christmas Prayer. Luke 2:36-39
- Prayer Beyond the Grave. Luke 16:2-31
- Prayer of a Troubled Soul. Luke 22:39-46 (Matt. 26:39-44, Mark 14:32-42, John 12:27-28, 18:1)
- Prayer of All Prayers. John 17:1-26
- Pray and Tell. Acts 4:23-31
- Prayer of The Unsaved. Acts 10:2-4, 9, 31
- Keeping First Things First. Romans 1:8-15, 10:1-2
- Praying God's Best for Others. Romans 15:5-6, 30-33, 16:24-27, II Corinthians 13:7
- Praying For the Church. Ephesians 1:15-20, 3:13-21

- <u>Praying for Spirit-Filled Living</u>. Ephesians 5:14-20
- <u>Praise and Purpose for Others</u>. Colossians 1:3-12
- <u>Prayer for a Finished Faith</u>. I Thessalonians 3:9-13, 5:16-24
- <u>Bound to Give Thanks</u>. II Thessalonians 1:3-5, 11-12, 2:13-17, 3:1-5
- <u>A Prayer to Remember Others</u>. II Timothy 1:3-18
- <u>The Spirit's Prayer</u>. Revelation 22:17-20 (See also 11:15-19, 19:1-10)

APPENDIX G: Teaching on Prayer (Selected Verses)

Be not rash with thy mouth, and let not thine heart be hasty to utter any thing before God: for God is in heaven, and thou upon earth: therefore, let they words be few. Ecclesiastes 5:2, Matthew 23:14

And he (Jesus) spake a parable unto them to this end, that men ought always to pray and not faint... Luke 18:1

And (Jesus) said unto them, Why sleep ye? Rise and pray, lest ye enter into temptation. Luke 22:46

- Sincerity in Prayer and A Pattern for Prayer. Matthew 6:5-18 (See also Luke 11:1-13)
- Asking with the Confidence of Faith. Matthew 7:7-11
- Praying to the Lord of the Harvest. Matthew 9:36-38
- Taking A Retreat to be Alone and Pray Matthew 14:23, Luke 5:16 and 6:12
- Praying in Agreement with Others and Its Power. Matthew 18:18-20, Acts 12:1-5 and following
- Mountain Moving Prayer by Asking, Believing and Receiving. Matthew 21:17-22
- Prayer that Goes with the Passover/Lord's Supper. Matthew 26:26-30
- The Benefit of Prayer—A rare glimpse of His Glory. Luke 9:28-36
- Persevering in Prayer. Luke 18:1-8
- The Hidden Power of Humility in Prayer. Luke 18:9-14
- Knowing Jesus Knew We Would at Times Fail and Yet He Has Prayed for Us. Luke 22:31-32
- Jesus' Prayer for Us as He Went to the Cross. John 12:23-32 (see Also

John 17:1-26)
- A Primary Job of Church Leaders. Acts 6:1-4 (see also 9:32-41, 10:2-4 and following, 16:9,13,16,25
- The Purpose of Jesus and the Power of the Spirit Found in Prayer. Romans 8:12-39
- An Expression of Ministry by All God's People to One Another. Romans 12:12, 15:30-33
- A Vital Part of Keeping Focus and Being Filled with The Holy Spirit. Ephesians 5:14-20
- A Powerful Weapon of Spiritual Warfare. Ephesians 6:18-19 (see also II Corinthians 10:4-7)
- Prayer as a Guardian Against Anxiety and Fear. Philippians 4:6-9, 13, 19)
- Praying For Ministries/Missionaries as a Regular Practice. Colossians 4:2-4, 12, 17
- Living in the Spirit of Prayer ("night and day"). I Thess. 3:9 (See also 5:16-18, 23-24)
- Praying that Others Be able to Live Worthy Lives. IIThess. 1:3, 11-12 (See also 2:13, 16-17, 3:1-5)
- Praying for People Who Have Done Evil to You to Be Likewise Rewarded. II Timothy 4:14-18
- Praying with Bold Confidence. Hebrews 4:16
- Observations about Jesus' Prayer Life. Hebrews 5:7-8 (see also 7:24-25)
- Praying for Wisdom. James 1:5-8
- What Causes Prayer to Go Amiss. James 4:2-3
- Praying for Healing. James 5:13-18 (see also Acts 28:8)
- Prayers and Married Life. IPeter 3:7-12
- When Thinking about the End Times—Pray! IPeter 4:7
- When You Need Restoration after a Period of Humble Suffering. I Peter 5:5-10
- When Quick Growth is Needed ("multiplied"). II Peter 1:2
- Assurance for What We Ask for in Prayer. I John 3:19-22 (see also 5:14-15)
- Being in the Spirit When You Pray. Jude 1:20 (see also Rev. 1:10)

- Temple Prayers Accompanied/Represented by the Smoke of Incense. Revelation 5:8 (see also 8:3)

Appendix H: A Possible Prayer Ministry

This approach is centered around the different people and places found in scripture where prayer occurs. Any similarity to other formal plans of a church prayer ministry model is purely coincidental.

I'd ask you to begin by reading Isaiah 43:18-19, *(18) Remember ye not the former things, neither consider the things of old. (19) Behold, I will do a new thing; now it shall spring forth; shall ye not know it? I will even make a way in the wilderness, and rivers in the desert.*

Philosophy of a Prayer Ministry

IMAGINE GETTING READY for next week's worship just after this week's worship and you turn to those around you and say, "Well I know we didn't have a lot of people here today to play or sing and some of it was not very focused or done well but if any of you know of some people, really anyone, that you can ask to show up next Sunday and lead us in worship that would be great." That likely doesn't happen, does it? Yet, I don't know of a single church that I've worked with that doesn't take that kind of attitude and approach to the ministry of prayer. Understand I'm not complaining I'm just explaining that the sad weakness we experience in churches around prayer comes from many problems. A pastor and/or people who are either unable (not trained) or unwilling (disobedient) to begin and continue a prayer ministry can be disheartening. We find ourselves without the competence, commitment, and courage to make prayer ministry happen the way that our inner spirit tells us that it should. Could it be that this attitude, so prevalent, is why our people and our churches are powerless and left wondering why? This is why I believe there is a better way.

Jesus indicated in Luke 18:1, "[people] ought always to pray, and not to faint". Likewise, Paul wrote in I Thessalonians 5:17-18, "Pray without ceasing.

(18) In every thing give thanks for this is the will of God in Christ Jesus concerning you." Paul further states in Philippians 4:16-17, "Be careful for nothing; but in every thing by prayer and supplication with thanksgiving let your requests be made known unto God." In addition, Paul's teaching about the armor of God that protects us is followed up by our one offensive weapon in Ephesians 6:18 where he says, "Praying always with all prayer and supplication in the Spirit, and watching thereunto with all perseverance and supplication for all saints; (19) And for me, that utterance may be given unto me, that I may open my mouth boldly, to make known the mystery of the gospel..." Do I really need to quote more scripture on the absolute imperative and necessity of prayer in the life of the individual and in the ministry of the church and its ministers? Can we agree that prayer as a discipline and as an ongoing ministry are foundational, essential, and non-negotiable as the heart and soul of the people of God? If you can't say yes, then this is where we likely part company. You're not serious. Perhaps there will be some, a remnant of God's people, who will think deeply on what prayer ministry should and could look like.

You see, I truly believe that there is a better way. Compare what we do in other ministries in our church and then think about how we treat prayer, and you will start to see a misaligned pattern of behavior. Our first example was related to worship. We value it for the power and impact it has on us as individual believers and as a group. Now, consider this—anyone can worship alone, and should, but only some *lead* us in worship, having differing responsibilities based on abilities, gifts, experiences, and leadership ability (ideally, the Pastor and music leader work together to craft a unified message). The music leader goes about working with the music, the musicians, vocalists, sound technicians, etc., to make that happen. In music, your absolute best days don't just happen by random people showing up. There is a plan. Let's get to the heart of it. If, for example, any person can lead someone to Christ (and even a pastor is encouraged to "do the work of an evangelist" II Timothy 4:5) but that does not mean that they have the gift or ministry of evangelist (think Billy Graham). In the same way we should view prayer ministry. Like Moses wishing that all of God's people were prophets (Numbers 11:29), we'd like it if all of God's people would pray. But that is not the way God usually organizes His people. So, what I'm suggesting and advocating is that we do something new. We begin not by asking people to join in on a prayer ministry out of pity but because of passion. I'm talking about a passion like when Jesus in Mark 11:15-19 is so fed up with the house of prayer being used for other purposes that He, the merciful and kind Jesus, turns over their tables and gets the church leaders of His day so upset that they are deciding how than can destroy Him! Are you passionate? Are you fed up with the status quo that never changes anything? Are you tired of starting a prayer ministry with a bang, limping along, then watching it die a slow agonizing death? I hope you are and are ready to do a New Thing!

Parts of A Prayer Ministry

PRAYER STARTS WITH the individual. You must start with someone who has an absolute passion for it and would be as dedicated to it as a minister/director/leader of any other ministry. Before you contact someone, make sure that they: (a) have a close walk with the Lord and they themselves obviously pray on their own, (b) have the capacity and experience to teach others how to pray, (c) are willing to create an ongoing ministry, and (d) are willing to build an organization where there is continuous training that will eventually be able to continue even if they are no longer present.

Potential Places

- The Mountaintop—Individual Prayer. (Mark 1:35; Luke 6:5-18). Individual prayer would be for any and all church members and would include an annual prayer conference, after which partner/members are encouraged to sign up for individual training/mentoring. Also, the event is followed up by daily/weekly prompts on prayer and prayer requests via printed and/or social media.
- The Garden—Staff/Leader (Elder/Deacon). Luke 22:39-46; John 17:1-26. Staff/leader prayer is a weekly (or every other) gathering of all staff and primary leaders ("elders" in some churches, "deacons" in others and both in some) hosted by the Pastor and Minister/Director of Prayer. Led by a rotation of all those in primary leadership roles. If you are a leader, you've shown you can lead. If you cannot lead the group in a devotional and then direct a season of prayer, then you are

actually not a leader. No offense. But you cannot as a leader expect the people to do what you yourself are not doing. Take it to heart. If your leadership is unable to do this, then train them. If your leadership is unwilling, discipline them or cut ties. That may seem harsh, but why would we not expect them to be leaders who pray and can train others to do the same? We teach what we know but we reproduce who we are! Don't let anyone off the hook—especially the pastoral staff and whoever is the primary leader of the Elder/Deacon group. No pray? Go away.

In addition, I think it is wise for each staff person to have an inner circle of prayer partners that they visit with and pray with (in person). Consider that Jesus had twelve disciples, but He also had Peter (Older), James (Close in age) and John (Younger) in His inner circle.

- The Upper Room. Acts 1:8-14; Acts 4:24-33. The Upper Room would be a feature for partner/member prayer as the body of Christ made up of two components: (1) Small Circle and (b) Corporate—All who wish to come. One of these could be done mid-week and the other on Sunday.
  - Small Circle. Led by the Inner Circle team of Minister/Director and Prayer Area Leaders. The purpose of this prayer time is targeted prayer, specific items given by Pastor, Staff, Elder/Deacon, etc.
  - Corporate. Led by Minister/Director and/or Prayer Area Leaders and/or Prayer Trainers. The purpose of this prayer time is to have general prayer, offered as a season of prayer

- The Watchmen. Isaiah 52:7-10(8); Isaiah 62:6; Isaiah 21:5-8; Jeremiah 6:9-17; 31:6; Ezekiel 33. A Watchman is a person with the expressed specific responsibility of being the person of prayer for a specific ministry or group. The Watchmen in ancient times stood upon the walls and in the towers in the city and could recognize a threat and sound the alarm and protect as needed. The ideal is not just to have a name of a Watchman, but to have someone who is *dedicated* to that area. Someone who is passionate about local evangelism or world missions or age group ministry is the person you're looking for. They may or may not be a director of that ministry. Ideally, they are specifically dedicated to the prayer over that ministry without also leading that ministry. You may have to slowly build this over time. Someone in the Inner Circle of the Prayer Ministry should organize, enlist, provide training information and provide a place for these Watchmen to pray.

- The Temple/ House of Prayer. Luke 2:37. This is the daily at-the-church-facility Prayer Ministry led by the Minister/Director of Prayer and/or an Inner Circle Partner. They lead a specific daily time for prayer at the facility attended by whomever may be there at the time and chooses to participate. These pray-ers are available for praying with and for those who drop by the facility during the church's working hours. One of these pray-ers could also, initially, take phone calls and emails related to those seeking prayer. As it grows, it would be best to have a dedicated person to field the calls, leaving the Director/ Minister of Prayer to be available to pray with those who stop by the building needing prayer.

- The Mercy Seat/The Altar. Hebrews 9:1-14 (esp. 3-5, 12-14); Exodus 25:22; Isaiah 53:1-6; 1st Kings 1:49-53. Another vivid picture in the scriptures is the top of the Ark of The Covenant. Annually, the High Priest would take the blood of a spotless lamb and spatter it upon the Mercy Seat whereupon the High Priest would declare the people of God to be sinless no more. In addition, in the Holy of Holies, no harm could be done to the one at the altar. In the same manner, we should have trained people to be available to counsel and pray with those seeking God's forgiveness and mercy as a response during a worship service. One of the Inner Circle should be the primary trainer and coordinate teams for each time of worship.

Partners of A Prayer Ministry

- Minister of Prayer/Director of Prayer Ministry. Directs the overall work. Leads the Inner Circle, trains others in training others on how to pray. Participates in daily prayer at the church facility and weekly events. Coordinates with Pastor and Staff for specific prayer items related to the overall ministry.
- Inner Circle. A small core of individuals dedicated to primarily (preferably) work only in the prayer ministry. If it is done well, it will likely take that much time and effort. You would not likely ask the leader of Music to do anything but music. If possible, the same should be done of those in the Inner Circle of the prayer ministry. The members of the Inner Circle will help in the application/interview process along with the Minister of Prayer to enlist and train people in the ministry of prayer. Lead in developing and coordinating prayer in the different ministries of the church (think worship, small group, men/women ministry, youth, children, evangelism, missions, etc.). More specifically, each person in the Inner Circle would have a specific area of the Prayer Ministry to lead and/or coordinate. The Watchmen (Ongoing Ministries), The Wall (Daily Prayer) and The Mercy Seat (Worship) would be assigned.
- Prayer Trainers. Must apply for and then be trained and seasoned before training others in how to pray. Must be involved in one of the primary parts of the prayer ministry to remain an official trainer. Prayer Trainers may also be looked at to build the inner circle.
- Prayer Partners. Individuals who may be trained but are not trainers. May or may not be Watchmen and seek to be involved regularly in the ministry of prayer as their primary function in the church. They would start with the understanding that they would at some point need to go through the training and be mentored by someone in prayer.

Space for the Prayer Ministry

THIS BRINGS UP THE necessity of having **dedicated space for the prayer ministry**—at least three spaces to start. First, a dedicated office is needed with access to phone, and a computer connected to the church where phone and/ or email items can be forwarded (that is not to say that a cell phone can't also be utilized but that is presumptive of the leader and their individual privacy rights). Second, a dedicated space for the actual praying, preferably near the office. This would be necessary in much the same way that we have a dedicated space for worship, children's ministry, etc. Is it a passion? A genuine priority? If it is, you'll be able to find the space and designate it for that specific use. Third, and this could be incorporated into the specific ministry space, a place large enough to have A Wall with all the ongoing requests and answers to prayer.

I want to give The Wall a little more specific emphasis. People know that we are a church that believes in praise, preaching, The Bible, and giving not only because of the specific acts of worship but also because of the potential for follow-up like listening to the songs or a live stream recording of the message. But what about prayer? I can't think of anything more moving about prayer than to see the The Wall in Jerusalem where there are people praying and putting prayers on paper and placing them in and on the wall. Having a visible place in the church like a wall in or near the foyer/sanctuary where anyone could stop, look, and participate in prayer would be a powerful tool to communicate that we believe in prayer. Again, a person from the Inner Circle would be responsible for reviewing and removing requests over time. A policy would need to be built about how the items get on the wall and who, and by what criteria, the items are removed and when/where/how results are reported.

www.ingramcontent.com/pod-product-compliance
Lightning Source LLC
Chambersburg PA
CBHW071828020426
42331CB00007B/1658